We're told in the Bible that Jesus never taught without a parable. There was a reason for that. Parables are powerful because they hold up a mirror and force us to see ourselves. I don't know many people who teach in parables today, but that's exactly what Jeremy Myers does in *Adventures in Fishing for Men*. He teaches with a parable that will challenge you to change your thinking, get out of your box, and actually become the "fisher of men" that Jesus has called you to become.

—Vince Antonucci
Author of *I Became a Christian and All I Got Was This Lousy T-Shirt*, *Guerrilla Lovers*, and *Renegade*
VinceAntonucci.com

Jeremy Myers' *Adventures in Fishing for Men* had me laughing so hard, I honestly forgot I was being taught. However, don't let the sheer entertainment value fool you. There's actually a profound message inside, and one today's church desperately needs to hear. We need to quit over-complicating the Great Commission and just go fishin'.

—Richard Jacobson
Author of *Unchurching: Christianity Without Churchianity*

Absurd, hilarious, and insightful! Jeremy Myers has crafted a fascinating tale with his incisive wit and boundless passion to point people toward greater fullness. You'll never view "fishing for men" the same way again, nor much else in your life either.

—Wayne Jacobsen

Author of *He Loves Me*, *Finding Church*,

and co-author of *The Shack*

Lifestream.org

Adventures in Fishing for Men is a funny, clever, and insightful description of how religion makes people relationally incompetent and spiritually superficial. It disarmed me with its humor while shining light on my self-righteous smugness. I highly recommend to anyone as an entertaining and meaningful read.

—Jimmy Wolfe

Director of Development, Camp Grace

Relentlessly funny and consistently brilliant, this book from Jeremy Myers is unlike anything else he's written before, but I'd certainly welcome more just like it. The extended allegory is hilarious and profoundly true all at the same time. Highly recommended.

—Keith Giles

Author of *Jesus Untangled: Crucifying Our Politics to Pledge Allegiance to the Lamb* and co-host of the Heretic Happy Hour Podcast

ADVENTURES IN FISHING FOR MEN

A HUMOROUS SATIRE OF CHRISTIAN EVANGELISM

JEREMY MYERS

RedeemingPress.com

ADVENTURES IN FISHING FOR MEN
A Humorous Satire of Christian Evangelism
© 2018 by Jeremy Myers

First edition, published 2012
Second edition, published 2018

Published by Redeeming Press
Dallas, OR 97338
RedeemingPress.com

ISBN: 978-1-939992-53-6 (Paperback)
ISBN: 978-1-939992-13-0 (Mobi Kindle)
ISBN: 978-1-939992-12-3 (ePub)

Learn more about Jeremy Myers by visiting RedeemingGod.com

Cover Drawing by Patrick Carlson

JOIN JEREMY MYERS AND LEARN MORE

Take Bible and theology courses by joining Jeremy at
RedeemingGod.com/join/

Receive updates about free books, discounted books, and new books by joining Jeremy at
RedeemingGod.com/reader-group/

TAKE THE ONLINE COURSE

There is an online course related to this book.
Each lesson contains an audio recording of a chapter,
some background information about where the ideas
came from, and several suggestions about how you can
truly become a "fisher of men."
Learn more at RedeemingGod.com/Courses/

The course is normally $197, but you can
take it for free by joining the Discipleship Group at
RedeemingGod.com/join/

Other Books by Jeremy Myers

Nothing but the Blood of Jesus

The Atonement of God

The Re-Justification of God: A Study of Rom 9:10-24

What is Prayer?

Christmas Redemption

Why You Have Not Committed the Unforgivable Sin

The Gospel According to Scripture (Forthcoming)

The Gospel Dictionary (Forthcoming)

Tough Texts on the Gospel (Forthcoming)

The Bible Mirror (Forthcoming)

The Grace Commentary on Jonah (Forthcoming)

Nin: A Novel (Forthcoming)

Studies on Genesis 1 (Forthcoming)

Studies on Genesis 2–4 (Forthcoming)

God's Blueprints for Church Growth (Forthcoming)

The Armor of God: Ephesians 6:10-20 (Forthcoming)

Books in the *Close Your Church for Good* Series

Preface: Skeleton Church

Vol. 1: The Death and Resurrection of the Church

Vol. 2: Put Service Back into the Church Service

Vol. 3: Church is More than Bodies, Bucks, & Bricks

Vol. 4: Dying to Religion and Empire

Vol. 5: Cruciform Pastoral Leadership (Forthcoming)

All books are available at Amazon.com

Learn about each title at the end of this book

To Sam Riviera
A truly great fisherman

TABLE OF CONTENTS

1. The Key to Fishing 11

2. My First Day on the Water 17

3. Stocking Up on Fish 21

4. Fishing Science 29

5. How to Attract Fish 37

6. The Fishin' Mission 45

7. My Trip to the River 49

8. Hooked on Fishing 53

9. An Expensive Lesson in Hooking 59

10. Letting Others Know You Fish 65

11. Fishing Rites 71

12. Meeting Fish Needs 77

13. The Fishing Channel 85

14. Attending the Fishing Club 93

15. Learning the Lingo 105

16. The Fishing Training Conference 111

17. The Fishing Prayer 121

18. Strategic Help In Training People to Love
    Angling Now 125

19. Fishing in Africa 131

20. World Fishing Training Center 137

21. The Fishing Covenant 143

22. Joe the Fisherman 151

23. The Fishing Charade 159

24. Becoming a Published Fisherman 167

Discussion Questions 173

About Jeremy Myers 205

CHAPTER 1

THE KEY TO FISHING

I want to become the world's greatest fisherman. I want people to talk about all the fish I caught, and the size of the monsters I pulled from lakes and rivers all over the world. I want to be interviewed in fishing magazines, be a guest on fishing shows, and get invited to speak at fishing conferences. I dream of the day that fishing methods get named after me and people interview me for their books about fishing.

The only problem with achieving this dream is that, so far, I haven't done any fishing.

So recently, I decided to get started.

But one cannot go out and just start fishing. One must prepare. Proper preparation is the key to fishing. A well-prepared fisherman is a successful fisherman.

You can quote me on that if you'd like.

So I went to the local fishing store and bought everything I thought I needed. I bought lures, flies, two poles, some fishing line, a creel, and a pair of needle-nosed pliers to remove the hooks from all the fish I was going to catch. I even splurged and bought myself a boat. After all, if you're going to fish, you should do it in style.

Never having fished before, I also knew that I needed to learn about fishing. If a well-prepared fisherman is successful, a teachable fisherman is even more successful. So I bought a few fishing magazines which looked like they could teach me something. However, being as humble and intelligent as I am, I knew that it would be foolish to actually read these magazines until I discovered what I needed to know about fishing. There is no sense learning about how to fish until I first learned the right questions to ask.

Besides, I was pretty sure I could figure out this whole fishing thing on my own. I mean, how hard could it be?

Furthermore, I didn't want to waste time reading and studying if I didn't need to. I had heard rumors of people who spent all their time reading about fishing, but who never actually got around to fishing. That wasn't going to be me.

So I put the fishing magazines in the boat with all of my other fishing gear. This way, if I ran into any problems while I was fishing, I could pull out a magazine and look for a solution.

The next day, once everything was set, I packed myself a lunch, and climbed into the boat.

What a beautiful day for fishing! The sun was out, a soft breeze whispered through the trees. The birds welcomed me with their song. I was well on my way to becoming the world's greatest fisherman.

"Nice boat," my neighbor said.

I hate it when people interrupt me when I'm trying to relax. And besides, I was just getting into this whole fishing thing. But I decided to be kind.

"Thanks," I said. "I bought it yesterday. I got a great deal. I bought the full package complete with a state-of-the-art fish finder and a leather captain's chair. And look, I bought top-of-the-line fishing poles and lures. All together, I only paid about $20,000, and I even got the salesman to throw in this hat for free."

He blinked when I said how much my gear had cost. Clearly he doesn't understand the high cost of fishing these days. Well, he's the foolish one. Sure, I paid a lot of money to get started, but I get to eat free fish for the rest of my life. He still has to buy his at the store. Maybe after I start catching boatloads of fish, I'll give him one every now and then.

"So where are you going to go fishing?" he asked.

I rolled my eyes and let out a sigh. The question didn't even make sense.

"I'm not *going* anywhere. I'm fishing here."

He looked at me strangely, and then looked around. He was obviously confused.

"You mean ... you're fishing *here*?"

"Yes. Isn't that what I just said?" He clearly was not a thinker. I pulled out a fishing magazine and pretended I was reading it.

He stared at me for another second or two, and then burst out laughing.

"You're not going to catch anything here," he said.

Oh, the audacity! The doubt! Besides, what does he know about fishing? He doesn't own a boat. I do. I bet he doesn't even have a rod. I waved my fishing magazine at him.

"I think I know what I'm doing. Look at all my magazines!"

He stared at me for a few seconds more. He was obviously trying to figure out how to refute my logic.

"Look," he finally said. "If you want to catch fish, you gotta put your boat in the water. You're never going to catch fish if you just keep it parked here in your driveway. Fish don't live in pavement."

Ack.

My retort froze in my throat as I glanced down at the fishing magazine in my hand. He might have a point. The cover showed a boat, decked out just like mine. But in the picture, the boat was sitting in the water. Mine was still in the boat trailer, parked in front of my garage. I had to think fast.

"Yeah, I know," I said. "I'm just getting ready to put it in the water … so I can go fishing … like in the magazine." I held up the magazine once more and pointed at the picture on the cover.

He shook his head, turned around, and walked into his house.

Sheesh. You have to explain everything to everyone these days.

CHAPTER 2

MY FIRST DAY ON THE WATER

We men know how to fish. It's in our blood.

It's instinct.

I'm like a king fisher, out here … fishing.

I could give lessons on fishing.

I could start a fishing club.

Maybe someday I will.

Once I become famous for my fishing prowess, fishermen from all over the world will come to me wanting to learn how to fish.

I wasn't a pro when I started. I made some mistakes. But I learned from them. Experience is the best teacher, after all. And now I am a professional. I am going to start catching lots of fish.

"Hey there, neighbor!"

Great. My pesky, know-it-all neighbor thinks he's so smart. Yesterday, he told me that in order to catch fish, I had to put my boat in the water. Like I didn't know that. But today I had nothing to fear: I had my boat in the water.

"Look!" I proudly pointed at the water under my fishing boat. "I've got my boat in the water!"

"Yes … Yes, you do." The words came slowly out of his mouth. What a dimwit. "And, uh … you bought a pool too, I see."

Why is this guy always criticizing me about how much money I spend? I'm the one trying to catch fish, and fishing is expensive. Besides, it was his idea to put the boat in the water.

"Well, duh!" I tried to say this nicely, but it's hard to be nice to someone who always insults you. "I had to put the boat in the water, and this was the best way to do it."

"Hmm …" He was clearly trying to decide what to say next.

Maybe I should ask him to help pay for my pool, since it was his idea. If he did, I suppose I could give him a fish or two when I caught them. No. They were my fish.

Then I had an idea.

"Hey, you want to get in? You can fish with me!"

"No … thanks for the offer though." He spoke slowly, cautiously, as though he was wary of my crushing intellect. "I don't think we'll catch any fish from your pool."

I laughed. "Yesterday you said I need to put my boat in the water, and today you say I don't. You need to be more consistent. This is why you lost your wife." I probably shouldn't have said that last part. But it was true. If he treated his wife the way he was treating me, it is no wonder they split up. Sometimes, people just need to be told the truth. And besides, I said it with love. You can say things like that if you say it with love.

But he didn't seem to appreciate my advice. His face got red and he clenched his jaw. But I didn't feel bad about what I said. People need the truth, whether they like it or not. I was about to say this to him, but he spoke first.

"Don't ever talk to me about my wife again," he said. His voice was calm and measured, but I sensed some seething rage beneath the surface. "You don't know anything about what happened between us." I was about to correct him on that, but he continued speaking, and I didn't want to interrupt. Interrupting is rude.

"And when I told you to put your boat in the water, I didn't mean a *pool*. Look down in the water. Do you see any fish? If you look through your stack of magazines there, you won't see anyone fishing in a swimming pool. If you want to catch fish, you have to go where the fish are. Fish live in lakes and rivers, so you gotta put your boat in a lake or a river." Then he turned away and walked off.

"Well, you should be more specific!" I yelled after him. "And besides, I knew that I wasn't going to catch fish in a pool. I'm just testing the boat for leaks!"

CHAPTER 3

STOCKING UP ON FISH

It was true what my neighbor said. When I looked through the magazines, all the pictures showed boats in rivers and lakes. But I had no intention of going fishing on a river or lake. I was kind of scared of water, and had used a pool because it was safer. If something happened, I could just jump out. Jumping out of a boat was not possible in a lake or river.

And fish could live in a pool, couldn't they? Why not? Water is water, right? Why couldn't I just go buy some fish, put them in my pool, and then fish for them?

Sure, it would defeat the purpose of catching all the free fish I could eat, because I would have to buy the fish before I caught them, but technically, if I bought them and set them free in my pool, and then caught them again, they were free fish. This is especially true if they reproduced in the pool! If they reproduced, I could keep my boat safely in the pool and still catch all the free fish I wanted.

The plan was genius. This was just another reason I was going to be a world-famous fisherman. Probably no one had ever thought of this before. Imagine the magazine articles that will be written about how I revolutionized the fishing strategies for fishermen everywhere!

But first I needed to prove that my idea worked.

So I went down to the pet store and asked to buy some fish. The pimple-faced teenager behind the counter asked what kind of fish I wanted to buy.

"One of each," I told him. "I'm a fisherman, and want to have experience catching many kinds of fish."

"Some of them are quite expensive," he said. "Are you sure you want one of each?"

He clearly didn't believe I was serious about fishing.

"No expense is too great for the avid fisherman," I answered. "Not only do I want one of each, but I will also need food for them. I want them to be well-fed. Also, I need them to reproduce. Fast. Do you have any tips on getting them to reproduce? Maybe some sort of special love potion for fish or something?"

"Well, for starters, you're going to need at least two of each fish. Maybe more. With some fish, we can tell which ones are male and which ones are female. Sometimes we can't tell until they start laying eggs."

I wasn't born yesterday. This kid was trying to scam me for sure. I had made the mistake of telling him that the avid fisherman spared no expense and now he was trying to sell me two of each fish! But I wasn't about to roll over that easily.

"This isn't my first time around the rodeo, sonny boy. I know what I'm talking about. Fish are fish, and they can mate with each other. I don't want to mate a fish with one of those parrots over there. I had dogs growing up, and a male dog can hump any female dog it wants." I felt bad about using such coarse language, but I had to make my point, and I couldn't allow myself to be pushed around by this punk kid.

I had noticed that this boy was wearing a crucifix, so I decided to quote Scripture at him.

"As the Bible says, 'God created each animal after its kind.' A dog is a kind of animal, and can mate with any other dog. A fish is also a kind, and can mate with any other fish. Telling me that a fish can only mate with fish that *look the same* is like telling me that white people can only mate with white people. That's racist. You're not racist, are you?"

He looked uncomfortable. This told me all I needed to know. He didn't realize I knew so much about fish, and he was now ashamed I had caught him in his attempt at extortion. To protect all future customers, I decided to put the fear of God in him.

"I'm thinking about calling over the store manager to tell him how you tried to steal my money. But I won't. You need to be honest from now on. You know where liars go, don't you?"

"Fine," he mumbled. "One of each it is."

"And some food too," I reminded him. "But just one big container is enough. They'll all be in the same pool."

He stared at me for a second.

"You can't put some of these fish together. They'll kill and eat each other if you do that. And fish go in an 'aquarium,' not a pool. Also, some of them need fresh water, and some salt water. And they don't all eat the same thing. Each fish needs different kinds of food."

This kid was really trying my patience. How can he be working in this store when he doesn't know anything about fish? Since he clearly was getting a terrible education in public school, I decided it was up to me to provide what his teacher and parents were not.

"You are just trying to steal my money again, and so in just a minute, I'm going to call the manager over and get you fired."

He started to stammer his objections, but I went on.

"There are four reasons I know you are lying. First, all these fish can be put together, because that's the way God made them. All water on earth is connected, right? Streams and rivers flow into lakes which flow into more streams and rivers until eventually, they all dump into the ocean. So they're all connected, and all fish are together. These guys will do just fine if I put them all in the pool.

"Second, when I said 'pool' I meant 'pool.' I don't care for your use of the fancy word 'aquarium.' If you want people to understand you, you need to speak the common, every-day language, and not use fancy words just to make yourself sound smart. Big words don't make you sound smart; they make you sound like a dumb person who is trying to sound smart. I am going to put my fish in a swimming pool, and that's what I'm going to call it—a pool. That way, my neighbor will understand what I'm talking about. If I called my pool an 'aquarium' he would give me that blank stare he always does when I say things that he doesn't understand. He's not very smart, just like you.

"Third, I already thought about the salt water. I saw a show on the Discovery Channel where some fish live in the ocean, and then they travel up fresh water rivers to mate and lay eggs. While I don't believe in evolution, I do believe that animals can adapt to changes in their environment, and so I think these fish can adapt. But to make it easy on them, I'm going to pour a couple containers of salt into my pool. This way, the pool will be half salty, somewhere between the saltiness of the ocean and the freshness of the lake. Both kinds of fish will adapt.

"Finally, I'm not going to buy any of your fancy-shmancy fish food. I was going to buy some, just to support your cause here, but now that you have tried to rob me two times, I'm not going to buy any food at all.

Fish in the lakes and rivers don't get special pet-store fish food and they do just fine. God provides them with all the food they need, and He will provide food for the fish in my swimming pool as well."

The kid just stared at me with his mouth slightly open. The look on his face was a lot like the look my neighbor gives me whenever I catch him in one of his illogical arguments. Now that I had corrected this kid in his faulty thinking, I had to do the difficult job of making sure he never took advantage of anyone else ever again.

"Go get your manager so he can fire you," I told him.

As the boy walked off he looked genuinely scared. It's too bad I had to give him this lesson in the harsh realities of life. Parents these days shelter their kids too much. The sooner a child learns the vital importance of honesty, integrity, and kindness, the better off they'll be. And they need to understand that if they aren't honest, trustworthy, and kind, they will suffer the consequences. If they don't learn these lessons when they're young, they could go to jail, end up murdered on the street, or worse yet, burn in hell for eternity. I always try to rescue such people, but they are usually too far gone by the time I meet them. I always wondered how people got that way.

But when the manager came over, I discovered why the boy was so ignorant, corrupt, and greedy. The manager supported and defended everything the kid had told me!

"I see where he learned his lies," I said. "So just sell me my fish, and I will be going. And trust me, I will never be back to this crooked pet store again. In fact, I'm going to tell all my friends to stay away from this place. I hope you go out of business!"

And wouldn't you believe it, when they gave me the fish—one of each from the entire store—most of the fish were smaller than my pinkie finger! They sold me baby fish! After the first few, I objected and told them that I wanted adult fish, but they said these tiny fish were full-grown! I know a full-grown fish when I see one, and these tiny minnows wouldn't provide a single mouthful for me, let alone a meal. But I know when to hold my tongue. Besides, baby fish would grow into adults. So even though I wasn't happy about it, I paid for the fish and left.

On my way out the door, I looked back over my shoulder and saw the two of them laughing. They probably charged me too much for the fish or something.

CHAPTER 4

FISHING SCIENCE

On the day after my trip to the pet store, I went out to my pool to see how my fish were doing. Every single one of them was dead.

It figures. Now I know why the store manager and that punk kid of his were laughing at me as I left. The fish they sold me were all sick! The crooks. I really should report them to the police. But I knew when to forgive and forget. Besides, didn't God say, "It is mine to avenge; I will repay"? I'll let God deal with them by sending them to burn forever in the pit of hell. That would be worse than sending them to prison where they might reform their lives and find Jesus. Yes, it was better to just let them continue in their sin. I had done my part. I had already warned the kid that he was headed for hell. His blood would not be on my hands as he burned for all eternity.

This still didn't solve my fish problem, though. What was I going to do about fish? I couldn't go buy more. My wife was already upset at how much I had spent on the boat, the fishing gear, the pool, and the fish. I couldn't spend more money right now. I had to find some free fish to put in my pool so I could begin catching them.

But where? Where could I find free fish?

I decided that maybe it was time to start reading some of those fishing magazines. I pulled a few out and started thumbing through them, looking for articles about where to find fish. And wouldn't you know it, there were several articles on this very topic! One article in particular was very helpful, stating that fish liked to hide under logs, behind rocks, and in the weeds. I had some of these right in my yard! Could it be possible that fish were hiding right in my backyard?

I didn't quite understand how this could be. Didn't fish live in water? How could they hide behind rocks and trees? Clearly, there was something I was missing. I hate it when scholarly articles like the one in this maga-zine leave out the most important details. The author acts like he's being helpful, but really, he's leaving out the most important information so he can keep all the fish for himself.

So I decided to put my superior research skills to work in finding a solution to this problem. The answer didn't take long. That's what happens when you have an intellect like mine.

I searched Google for "fish on land" and learned that scientists have discovered a fish that climbs out of the water and walks around on land. They call it a "mud skipper." At first I thought this was just an attempt by pagan scientists to prove evolution. A few years ago I had been tricked into thinking that the jackalope was real, and I wasn't about to make *that* mistake again.

So to verify the information about the mud skipper, I called a guy from church who was a scientist. I have always doubted whether he was really a Christian or not, because he went to a secular university for his education where they taught him evolution. But he claimed to believe in creationism, so I hoped the university hadn't tainted his mind too bad and he wouldn't give me any evolution malarkey.

When I asked him about the mud skipper, he confirmed it was real. But when I asked him if other fish could also walk on land, he said they couldn't. It just goes to show you, I guess, that even Christian scientists who believe in creationism don't know everything. Those pagan universities really mess people up.

By my reasoning, if one fish can climb out of the water and walk on land, others could too. That is the way God's creation works. And if scientists didn't think other fish could do this, this is just because they haven't discovered it yet. After all, scientists used to think that the earth was flat. Eventually, I am certain that scientists will discover that all fish can climb out of the water and walk on land, just like the mud skipper. The reason it hasn't been discovered yet is because the fish are good at hiding behind the rocks and trees, just like it said in that magazine article. Furthermore, there was that famous saying, "Like a fish out of water." Clearly, this meant that fish could live out of water, or else why would it be a saying?

My logic was flawless. I now knew that I did not have to buy fish from the pet store, or go down to the rivers, lakes, and streams to get fish. All I had to do was lure the fish out from behind the rocks and trees and into my swimming pool. *Lure* was a fancy fishing word I learned while reading the fishing magazine. It just means "attract." I don't know why scholars like to use fancy words that nobody else uses, but I'm smart enough to know what he meant by the word *lure.*

Anyway, the fact that science hadn't yet discovered that all fish can live on land means that once I figure out how to lure the fish out, I could write books about it, and maybe become as famous as Christopher Columbus who had discovered the earth was round! This just goes to show you that God blesses those who work hard and use their brains.

But before I could lure the fish into the pool, I knew I had to make sure the pool looked attractive and welcoming to the fish. If fish liked to hide behind rocks and trees, then they probably wouldn't come out of their current hiding spots and get into my pool unless it had rocks and trees in it as well.

I thought about just picking up some of the rocks and digging up some of the trees in my yard and tossing them into the pool, but I was afraid that this might scare aware the fish that might be hiding under them. So I asked my wife if I could go buy some rocks and trees at the local landscaping store, but when she found out what they were for, she said no. Women just don't understand what it takes to be a fisherman.

So as I was sitting in my boat mulling over this problem of where to get rocks and trees, I looked over into my neighbor's yard and saw that he had a bunch of rocks lying all over the place and several small trees growing here and there. I bet he wouldn't mind if a borrowed a few.

I was almost done when my neighbor came storming out of his house. I had never seen him so angry. "WHAT THE HELL ARE YOU DOING?!" he yelled at me. "YOU JUST TORE UP ALL MY LANDSCAPING!"

I hate it when people use foul language in my presence. Don't they know how offensive and rude it is? But I have learned that in these situations, you have to respond calmly so the situation doesn't escalate. After all, the Bible says that "A gentle answer turneth away wrath."

"You better be careful with that language," I replied. "Or you'll be going to hell. And the yelling shows that you have an anger issue. Anyway, I'm just borrowing a few rocks and trees for a few days. I'll give them back when I'm done."

He stared at me with his eyes bulging. A vein on his neck looked like it was about to pop. "You're *borrowing* my trees and rocks? What for?"

I motioned over to my pool where the branches of several trees stood out from the surface of the water. "I'm making my pool more attractive for fish. Once I get some fish in the pool, and they grow accustomed to being there, I will give all the trees and rocks back. Then you can put them back wherever you want again."

"First of all," he growled, "You probably just killed my trees. They can't handle that much water, especially if it's chlorinated water. Secondly, what do you mean, 'you can put them back'? You took them without asking me … shouldn't you be the one to put them back? And finally, look at the mess you've made of my yard. Are you going to fix that?"

The nerve of this guy! It sure is hard being neighborly these days. "The trees will be fine." I said. "As everybody knows, trees need water to grow. I'm giving them lots of water, so they'll probably be healthier than ever.

And it's not chlorinated because that would kill the fish. Second, I can't put the trees and rocks back because I'm not a landscaper; I'm a fisherman. But it will be easy for you to put them back because I left all the holes in your yard where they go. Third, if anyone should be upset, it's me. Look at what all the dirt from the rocks and roots did to the water of my pool. It looks like a big mud puddle now. Do you know how long it will take for my water filter to clean out all that mud?"

As I patiently explained these things to him, I could see he was getting angry again. So I tried to ease his concern. "Look. Next time I promise to not dig up your trees. And I'm sorry about not asking. I didn't want to bother you. But you're here now, and I still need more trees. Can I just cut off the top three or four feet of the trees that are still in your yard? They'll grow back."

"CUT OFF THE TOP OF MY TREES?!" he was back to yelling now. "NO! And trust me; there won't be a next time! Keep the rocks and trees you stole from me! I don't want you stepping foot in my yard again!" With that, he stormed back into his house and slammed the door. Some people are so rude.

CHAPTER 5

HOW TO ATTRACT FISH

Early the next morning, I set my intellect to work at figuring out how to lure fish into my swimming pool. Although I had discovered that all fish can climb out of the water and hide behind rocks and trees and had filled my swimming pool with rocks and trees to make it look welcoming for fish, I still had to figure out how to lure them into my swimming pool.

But what was all that noise? I could hardly think because of the racket coming from outside. I stepped outside to see what was happening, and there was my neighbor, building a fence between his house and mine. He was cutting the boards with a table saw and then nailing the fence together.

"Hey!" I yelled at him. "Why are you building a fence? When people put up fences, it keeps us all separate from each other. There can't be true community when there are fences!" But he just ignored me and kept building.

"Besides," I continued, "You're scaring away all the fish and I need them to get into my pool!" Still no response.

"Well, just make sure the fence looks good!" I shouted over the noise. "A nice fence is better to look at than your torn-up backyard!"

I decided to go back inside after that. I don't think he was going to hit me with that hammer in his hand, but the glare in his eyes made me nervous. This is why the world is going the way it is. First, people shut themselves off from their neighbors with fences, and the next thing you know, they're killing each other with hammers.

Once I was back inside, I put in some earplugs and got down to the business of thinking about how to attract fish. I remember one of my magazines had an article about thinking like a fish. I had dog-eared the page to read later, and figured it would be pretty helpful right now. But I decided to skip the article for now. I was pretty confident in my ability to solve this problem on my own. Besides, the magazines were out in the boat, and I would have to see my neighbor again if I went out to get one.

So I put my mind into high-gear, and got to work. As I expected, the solution did not take long. First, I asked myself why I did not already know how fish thought. The answer to this question was that I was not

a fish. I am glad that God did not make me a fish. Fish
are slimy and gross. And they die easily. I still cannot
believe all those fish I bought from the pet store died in
my pool. They were starting to stink too. I left them in
the pool so they could be food for the other fish that
climbed in there. Fish were like that. They feed on each
other. It just goes to show you how depraved they are.

Anyway, it was when I realized I was not a fish that I
found my answer. The reason I did not understand fish
was not just because I was not a fish, but because fish
lived in a whole different environment than I did. I
lived in the air. They lived in the water. I read books
and magazines. They just swam around doing fish
things like reproducing and eating. In a way, fish are
from another world.

I am not saying fish are aliens, for we all know that
God didn't create any aliens anywhere else in the uni-
verse. If He had, He would have told us so in the Bible.
But since humans live on ground and fish live in water,
it is kind of like fish are from a different world.

That is when it dawned on me. When I was young-
er, I watched the movie E.T., and in it, the little boy
lured an alien into his room by laying out a line of
Reese's Pieces. I don't think they sell Reese's Pieces anymore, but even if they did, I don't know if fish like
them. But I did know from reading my magazines that
fish liked worms, flies, and grasshoppers.

So to lure the fish out from behind the rocks and trees, all I had to do was put out a line of worms, flies, and grasshoppers, leading from behind each rock and tree in my yard, and into the pool. The fish would come out of hiding, just like E.T., and then follow the line of bugs until they plopped into my pool. It was a genius plan.

Except for one thing: I didn't have any worms, flies, or grasshoppers. And I wasn't sure how to get any. I had noticed that flies had begun to buzz around my swimming pool due to the rotting fish, but there was no way of getting these flies to stand in a line from the rocks and trees up to my pool.

But this minor setback was not too much of a problem for me. When life gives you lemons, make lemonade. So I decided that the flies around my pool were actually helpful. All I had to do was tell the fish that there were flies at my pool, and whole schools of fish would show up. Clearly, if I told the fish that my pool was full of water and had lots of flies buzzing around, they would leave their hiding places and come to the pool.

Then I also realized that it wasn't just flies. My pool also had worms! When I was digging up the rocks and trees from my neighbor's yard, I had noticed several worms wriggling around in the dirt that was stuck to the roots of the trees. So my pool had everything a fish needs! All I had to do was invite them!

So I made up several signs with pictures of worms, flies, and grasshoppers on them, and also put a picture of my pool on each sign. Then I put these signs in strategic locations where fish were sure to see them. When the fish got hungry, they would see the signs, and would leave their hiding places and get into my pool.

I did feel a little guilty about the grasshopper signs. Since I didn't actually have any grasshoppers, the signs weren't quite truthful. But I figured that eventually I would find some grasshoppers, and I would dump them into the pool as well. So the signs weren't dishonest; they were a promise of good things to come. It would give the fish something to look forward to as they feasted on worms and flies. The fish would be so happy, I bet they would invite some of their fish friends into the pool as well.

It took me about a week to make the signs. Then I put them up around my yard and even nailed a few to my neighbor's new fence. Then I sat back and waited. So far, no fish have shown up, but these things take time. After all, fishing requires a lot of patience, and I am a very patient person.

"Hey, neighbor!"

"AAAGH!" I yelled. "You scared me!"

He was peering at me over the top of his fence and looking around my yard at all the signs. "Don't worry," he said. "I'm not carrying a hammer today."

"Ha!" I laughed shakily. "I only got scared because I didn't see you walking up. You know … because of the fence."

"Listen," he said. "I don't know if you've noticed, but your pool is emitting a terrible stench. I am trying to re-landscape my yard, and I can't hardly breathe out here because of the smell. I think it's because of all those dead fish you have floating around in there. If you want, I can come over and help you clean your pool."

"It only stinks because you don't know anything about fishing," I answered. "I need the fish to rot so that they attract flies, which will in turn attract more fish. The new fish will eat the flies and the dead fish, because that's how fish are. Then the smell will go away. See the signs all over my yard? It's all part of my fishing plan. The smell is a sacrifice a true fisherman has to make if he wants to catch fish."

He looked at me for a while and started to get that crazy look in his eyes. But I wasn't worried, because he wasn't carrying a hammer. Finally, he sighed, and said, "You know, there are different and better ways of catching fish. Lots of people catch fish every day, and it doesn't ruin the neighborhood or stink up our yards."

I rolled my eyes, shook my head, and took a deep, calming breath. "I am a fishing expert and I know what I'm talking about. You don't. I have never seen you do anything remotely associated with fishing. If you did fish, you would know that this is the smell of fishing. Besides," I said, "you're rarely at home anyways and so the smell shouldn't bother you."

He looked at me for a minute, seeming like he wanted to say something. He was probably trying to figure out how to refute my irrefutable logic. But he finally just shook his head, turned around, and walked back into his house.

CHAPTER 6

THE FISHIN' MISSION

While I waited for fish to come out from hiding and visit my pool, I decided to begin training myself about how fish think. I had read about this in a magazine and knew it was important. I figured the best way to do this was to go where the fish lived.

I knew enough about fishing now to know that most fish lived in lakes, rivers, and streams. I certainly wasn't going to live near one of these bodies of water, but it wouldn't hurt to take a tour of one. I even came up with a fancy name for my excursion: I called it my "Fishin' Mission." There was a river not too far from me, and I decided to go there for my first trip.

I must confess that in the back of my mind I had plans for more than just seeing the river and learning about fish. In one of my magazines I read about "Fishing Tours" and decided that once I became a world-famous fisherman, I could charge people to go down to the river with me where they could take pictures and learn from me about the dangers of rivers and the joys of fishing. Then they could go home and tell everybody about the river and show people pictures. Some of those people would want to come on the tour, and I could have a steady source of income. It would be great.

But first things first. Before my Fishin' Mission could become world-famous, I needed to get some actual experience going down to the rivers and lakes to learn about all the fish I was going to catch. I was a little too scared to go alone, however, so I decided to invite some other people to go along with me. This would be beneficial in two ways.

First, I had heard somewhere that there is no such thing as a "Lone Ranger Fisherman." I think this means that no fisherman should fish alone but this explanation didn't really make sense to me because the Lone Ranger had Tonto. Regardless, I figured it was good advice, and needed to find some people to go with me. When you are going to someplace as scary as lakes and rivers, there is strength in numbers.

The second reason I wanted to find some others to go with me is that they would be good PR. Once they came back with adventure stories of our time on the river, with pictures of the giant fish we caught, and tales of the monsters that got away, I would have people beating down my door to go on a Fishin' Mission with me. All I needed to do was get a few people to go with me the first time, and then word of mouth would do the rest.

So I made up some flyers and stapled them on telephone poles and fences around town. Nobody called. So I plastered the flyers on the walls of some businesses in town and put them in the windshields of cars. I did get one call on those, but it was from the police telling me that they had received some complaints and if I did this again, I would get fined for littering.

Since my ad campaign wasn't working, I decided to use the personal touch. I went door-to-door in my neighborhood to see if anybody wanted to join me. I must have talked to over a hundred people, but nobody seemed very interested in going with me. People are too selfish and lazy.

I even went to my neighbor's house, but he wasn't at home. His wife answered, and she seemed flustered by her children crying in the background, the phone ringing, and something on the stove which smelled like it was burning. I know that life is busy, but she didn't have to so rudely slam the door in my face when I asked if she could get her children to calm down while I explained my mission to her. It was impossible to think while they were crying. I will have to speak to my neighbor about his parenting skills and his wife's attitude after he gets back.

So I didn't get anybody who would agree to go with me. I did, however, get a few people from the neighborhood to commit to praying for me. As I talked with people, I told a story from one of my fishing magazines about a man who went fishing and got eaten by a crocodile. I think that is why they offered to pray for me. This Fishin' Mission was going to be dangerous.

CHAPTER 7

MY TRIP TO THE RIVER

Since no one would go with me to the river, I decided to go by myself.

But when I got down to the river, things didn't go quite as planned. First of all, the bank was steep and I fell a few times on my way down to the water. But once I got down there, I discovered that the river was more dangerous than I ever imagined. The water was moving! I had heard rumors that people actually got into the river to fish, but I knew by looking at the water rushing by that nobody would be that foolish. Even if they survived, how would they ever get home?

Just as I was thinking these thoughts, I looked up the river and saw a boat floating down the river toward me, and inside were some fishermen! At first I thought these men were fearless, but as they floated closer, I realized they were just foolish.

They were unwashed, sweaty men, with facial hair. Such burly, scruffy men should not be allowed to be fishermen. They give fishermen a bad name.

And the language they used was even worse. It sounded like they were trying to kill the fish with their foul mouths. I immediately concluded that these were not *true* fishermen, but were frauds. They were false fishermen who only gave the appearance of fishing. Fishermen were like me. We have dignity, style, and can craft a flowery tale about the fish we've caught. Resorting to such coarse language as they did is only proof of a weak mind. They clearly hadn't read all the books that I had about proper fisherman etiquette.

Then one of them took a big swig from a can of beer! I shook my head in disbelief. No wonder these fakers were out here. They weren't even fishing. They probably told their wives they were going fishing, but actually just came out here to get drunk and tell coarse jokes. As they floated off down the river, I was glad to see them go, and hoped that the river swept such false fishermen out to sea.

Walking further down the shore, I met some young boys who were also fishing. They were fishing from shore, throwing their lines into the water and then reeling them back in. I laughed to myself. It's always humorous to watch little boys play. They clearly didn't know what they were doing since they couldn't cast their line right the first time. They kept casting it out, and reeling it in. Casting it out, and reeling it in. It looked like a lot of work, and for what? With all that work, the fish were sure to be scared away.

I tried to explain to them that fishing should be relaxing. That all you have to do is put your line in the water, then let it sit there. While you wait for the fish to come to you, you can sit back in your boat, relax, and read a good book. These young boys didn't even have a boat.

"I don't like to read, Mister," said the boy closest to me. "And when I do, I don't understand much of what I read."

"There's your first problem," I told him. "To be a good fisherman, you should read some books about fishing, and subscribe to some fishing magazines. The more you read and know about fishing, the better fisherman you will be."

They seemed to understand what I was saying, and asked if I had caught anything yet.

"No," I said. "I'm just surveying the river today, looking for a good place to fish." As I started to walk on by, it looked like one of them got his hook caught on the bottom of the river. His pole bent over, and the reel started making a whizzing noise.

"I got one! I got a fish!" the kid yelled.

Poor kid. He gets his line stuck on a log, and thinks it's a fish. But he started to try to reel in the log anyway, and it turned out to be a fish after all!

I think I got more excited than the kid. I had never seen a real, live fish caught in the wild before. I was jumping around and hollering and just about fell into the river. I asked if I could hold the fish.

"Sure," said the kid. And he handed the fish to me. But as soon as I touched it, it wriggled and slipped out of my hands, landed back in the river, and swam quickly back into the depths of the water.

The boy was upset, and I felt a little bad as I walked away. But he was too young to know what to do with a live fish anyway. I mean, if I didn't know what to do with it, how could he?

My hands reeked of fish for hours afterwards, and I realized that if I was going to be a fisherman, I needed to figure out how to do it without touching any fish.

CHAPTER 8

HOOKED ON FISHING

After watching the boys catch a real, live fish on the riverbank the day before, I decided that I better learn how to cast my line into the water like they were doing. That's the thing with fishing. You can only learn so much from magazines. At some point, you have to follow the example of others and let them teach you their secrets. The boys didn't know it, but I had been watching them pretty closely and was certain I could master their technique in no time at all.

So I got out my fishing pole and on the end of the line, tied the best hook from my tackle box. It was a big hook, almost two inches long, with a big, sharp barb on the end. I bought the biggest hook they had down at the fishing store because I knew I would be catching some big fish. Those boys had been using a small hook, and as a result only caught small fish. This giant hook of mine was sure to catch the biggest fish around.

I pulled the fishing rod back over my shoulder and was just about to swing it forward when my neighbor stepped out of his house.

"Hey there, neighbor!" he shouted. "What's going on?"

I sighed to myself. Can't this guy ever mind his own business?

"I'm practicing my casting technique," I told him.

"Oh," he said. "I thought maybe you were trying to fish again, but this time in your grass!" He laughed at his joke. I did not.

"For your information," I replied, "I went down to the river yesterday and had a very successful day."

"You mean you caught some fish?" He looked genuinely surprised.

"I had a big fish in my hands, but I let him go." This wasn't a lie. Sure, the boy caught the fish, but I did hold him in my hands, and the fish did go back into the river. But these were minor details which would take too much time to explain. Right now I had to practice my casting.

"How big was this fish?" my neighbor asked.

I get so tired of all his questions. I sighed, loud enough for him to hear. Hopefully he would get a clue.

"It wasn't as big as the fish I am going to catch," I said. "Look at the size of this hook." I walked over to

him and showed him the giant fishing hook I had tied
to the end of my line.

He looked shocked. "You're going to go fishing with
that? Where will you be fishing? The ocean?"

I just laughed. This was the oldest trick in the book.
I now understood why he was asking all these questions.
He was trying to get me to reveal my secret fishing spot.
Little did he know that I didn't have one yet. But I
didn't need to tell him that. Let him think I had found
a secret fishing hole with giant fish in it. I was a master
fisherman, and when I came home with the monster of
a fish, he would see. Then maybe the questions would
stop.

"I'm not telling you where my secret fishing spot is,"
I said. "Right now, I'm just practicing my casting."

"With that hook? I don't know if that's a good idea.
Especially not with that little rod you've got. Even if
you were to catch a fish with that hook, it would snap
your line or break your rod. And besides, you don't really need a hook on your line to practice casting. Especially not one with that barb. That thing is wicked!"

"No, liars and thieves are wicked," I said. "Fishing
hooks are morally neutral." We who know the difference between good and evil must do our best to inform
others that sin and wickedness is nothing to joke about.
He apparently understood my point, and said nothing.
So I continued.

"Now, stand back and watch the master fisherman practice his casting."

He stepped back, and I pulled the rod back over my shoulder the way I had seen the boys do the day before. Then I swung the rod forward with all my strength, just as I had seen the boys do.

A sharp pain stabbed through my ear!

"CRAP!" I screamed. That was the strongest cuss word I allowed myself to say. I was very disciplined. The giant hook, rather than sail gently through the air to land on the other side of the lawn, had lodged itself in my right ear. I fell to the ground in pain and reached up to see if I could dislodge the hook. I pulled on the hook and screamed again.

"CRAP! It hurts!"

"Here, let me help!" my neighbor said as he ran over.

I was furious at him. This was all his fault, really. If he hadn't interrupted my first cast, none of this would have happened. So when he got to me, I tried to push him away.

"I don't need your help. I can do it myself!" But as I hastily reached out with the hand that was holding my ear, the hook pierced right through my thumb as well.

I screamed in agony.

"Look what you did!" I yelled at my neighbor. There was blood running down my forearm and dripping onto my expensive fishing vest. "You interrupted my casting, and now my ear and thumb are stuck with this hook. And my vest is getting stained with blood!"

He looked pretty angry and started walking toward me. I thought he was going to hit me, but then he pulled a knife out of his pocket. I started to scramble away, thinking he was going to stab me. I knew my neighbor was a sinner, but I never imagined that he was a murderer.

But he came up, grabbed me, and said, "Hold still. I'm going to cut the line to the fishing rod then take you to the hospital. You're going to need a doctor to take that hook out."

He helped me get into his car, and on the way to the hospital, I purposefully dripped a little blood onto the seat of his car. It wasn't a nice thing to do, but all of this was his fault anyway, and he still hadn't even apologized.

When we got to the hospital he stayed with me the entire time while the doctor cut the barb off the hook, put some topical anesthesia on my thumb and ear, and then pulled the hook free.

After I was all bandaged up, my neighbor drove me home. He never did apologize, and didn't even offer to pay the medical bill. But at least he didn't ask any more questions.

I did learn one thing from this experience: In the future, whenever I practice my casting, I am going to make sure that my neighbor is not at home.

CHAPTER 9

AN EXPENSIVE LESSON IN HOOKING

After the trouble with the hook, I decided that I needed some lessons on handling hooks. All aspects of fishing can be divided up into specialties. Just as one company specializes in making the poles, and another specializes in making the reel, so also one fishing instructor might specialize in casting while another specializes in all things related to hooks. Sure, there were generalists who could teach the basics of fishing, but if you really want to learn from the best, you have to find the specialists.

At least, this is how I *think* it works.

Since I needed help with hooks, I didn't want a jack-of-all-trades fishing instructor. I needed the best of the best. I needed someone who specialized in the proper use of hooks. I knew that such a person existed because I had recently overheard some men talking about a really good *hooker* that they had found. I wasn't sure how to find a hooker, but decided that the place to begin was at the local fishing store.

The lady behind the counter looked shocked when I asked her if they had any hookers I could hire for the day. Maybe she thought I couldn't afford such specialized training.

"I'll pay whatever it costs," I told her. "I want only the best."

"I ... I ... I'm sorry," she stammered. "Women like that don't work here."

I don't know why I always seem to get the incompetent employees at these stores.

"I don't want a woman. I want a man. Everybody knows that men are the best hookers." I am not sexist, but I have never heard of a good fisher*woman*. It's fisher*men* for a reason.

I wasn't going to get anywhere with this woman, so I asked to speak to the manager. I had learned from the fish store incident that when I was faced with an ignorant employee, the best thing to do was ask for the store manager. When he came over, I repeated my request.

"I want to hire a hooker. And not a beginner either. I want an experienced professional."

The manager looked just as flustered as the clerk.

"I'm sorry," he said. "Women like that don't work here."

Sometimes, you just have to educate people. This was one of those times.

"I tell you, women's rights have ruined this country. I know there was the whole women's liberation movement in the 60s, which gave women the right to be CEOs and Senators and hookers, but I'm sorry, enough is enough! Call me old fashioned, but I want a top-quality male hooker!" I probably raised my voice a little too much because people were staring at me, but I didn't care. People need to know when they're wrong.

Apparently the manager was one of those leftist, communist liberals who thought women could do any job as well as a man, because he asked me to leave the store before he called the police. I bet he wouldn't have done that if I had asked for a female hooker. But rather than argue, I decided to leave.

On the way out the door, a stranger came up to me and handed me a scrap of paper.

"Here's what you need," he said. And then he walked away. I looked at the paper. On it was a phone number. Just when I had started to lose hope in humanity, a stranger showed some kindness.

I called the number as soon as I got home. A man answered.

"I'm looking for a hooker," I told him. "The best you've got."

"Sure. What are you looking for? Blonde? Brunette? Redhead? Russian? Asian?"

Was this guy crazy? Why is he asking me about hair color and race?

"It doesn't matter," I told him. "Whoever is best. How much will it cost?"

"That depends on how long you want," he said. "Our best hooker is $500 an hour, but there are multi-hour discounts if you want her for longer."

"Her?! I was told I could get a man. And $500? That's a lot of money!"

"Well, believe me, the services we provide are worth every penny. And we do have men, but they are all out with other clients right now. I can book an appointment for tomorrow if you'd like."

I sighed. "I really need someone today because I'm going fishing tomorrow. If the women are just as good, go ahead and send a woman."

"I'll send our best right away," he answered. "Make sure you have the money ready. She'll be at your house in about half an hour."

I now understood why it cost so much money. This was prompt service, and the hooker was coming to my house!

Half an hour later, a car pulled into my driveway. The woman who got out was not at all what I imagined. She certainly was not dressed for fishing. I blushed just looking at her. The skirt was definitely too short. She walked to the door and knocked.

I opened the door and greeted her. I noticed that all she was carrying a little handbag.

"Where's your pole?" I asked.

She smiled. "I'm not a dancer, honey. But I bet you've got a pole I could use. Do you have the money?"

I gave her $500 and told her that if she was good, I would hire her for additional hours later.

That's when things got strange. She came up and started unbuttoning my shirt! I know I'm handsome, but I'm a married man, and I told her so.

"Most men I work with are married," she said, as she continued to unbutton my shirt. "But it's okay. It'll be our little secret. I am very discreet."

I calmly tried to explain to her what I wanted.

"Look. I hired a hooker because I just want someone to show me how it's done. I tried it the other day, and I got hurt pretty bad." I showed her the bandages on my finger and my ear. That got her attention, and she stopped trying to remove my shirt.

"I can do some kinky stuff if you want," she said. "But that's extra."

"I know that tying knots are involved," I told her. "But I am not sure I want kinks in my line. Right now I just want to learn the basics. This is my first time."

She looked thoroughly confused. "Aren't you married?" she said. "How can this be your first time?"

Now I was the one who was confused.

Right then, my wife walked in the door and after a few seconds of shocked silence, the yelling started. I am still not really sure what all the fuss was about, and I think my wife overreacted, but one thing is certain, I will never hire a professional hooker again.

And wouldn't you believe it, the hooker took my $500 with her when she left, and I didn't even get my lesson!

CHAPTER 10

LETTING OTHERS KNOW YOU FISH

As I continue my quest to become the world's greatest fisherman, I have discovered that success is not measured in how many fish you actually catch, but in how well you present yourself as a fisherman. This was a great relief to me, because the more I learn about fishing, the less I like it. Some days, I am pretty sure I hate fish. They stink, they are slimy, and those bugged-out eyes kind of freak me out.

Thankfully, you don't have to catch fish to be a world-famous fisherman. All you have to do is project the image of being a successful fisherman and be able to teach others how to fish. There are two kinds of fisherman: those who fish, and those who teach others to fish. I am one of the latter.

But before people will listen to you about how to fish, you have to convince them that you are a great fisherman. How is this possible if, like me, you have never actually caught fish? There are numerous ways.

The first thing I did was buy a fishing necklace with a hook on it. I made sure the hook on my necklace was plastic, of course. I didn't want to risk any more trips to the hospital. I made sure the hook was fluorescent pink, and I wore it on the outside of my shirt so that everybody could see it as I walked around.

I felt pretty good about making such a public statement that I was a fisherman, but one day I saw a guy wearing a golden fishing hook. It looked very expensive, and when I asked him about it, he said it was *real* gold! Clearly he was a better fisherman than I was because he was wearing a golden hook and mine was cheap plastic. I immediately went out and bought myself the biggest, brightest, and most expensive golden fishing hook I could find. Now, everywhere I go, people look with admiration at my fishing hook necklace. The amazement is obvious on their faces about what a great fisherman I am.

Another great way to show people that I am a fisherman is by wearing fisherman t-shirts. I have one t-shirt that says, "If you were to die tonight, do you know where you would fish for eternity?" Another that I wear a lot says, "Fish with Jesus on streams of living water ... or try your luck at the lake of fire." The choice is obvious. I find that wearing shirts like this really help me feel like a true fisherman.

Also, bumper stickers are nice. My favorite bumper sticker, which I placed on both my cars and on the back of my fishing boat, reads, "Love the fish; hate fish guts." I have often thought that fish would be much better if they didn't have any guts. I have watched some videos about cleaning fish, and while I have never actually done it myself, it looks disgusting. I think that fish guts are actually what keeps me from catching any fish. I would not want to deal with their guts.

Another favorite bumper sticker of mine says "My Boss is a Jewish Fisherman." That's a reference to Jesus, in case you didn't know. He was quite the fisherman. Of course, He had an advantage over the rest of us, being God and all. Nevertheless, He gave some good fishing advice, and I try to follow everything He said when I go catch fish. Or at least, I *will* follow all His advice when I go catch fish. Right now, I am just spending lots of time reading and studying what He said so that I can be well-prepared to catch fish when I actually get out there and do it.

Along with the fishing necklace, t-shirts, and bumper stickers, it is also wise to buy lots of fishing magazines and fishing books. But don't worry; you don't have to actually read them. You just need to make sure these books are visible so that people *think* you're reading them. If you line your shelves with these books and magazines and put a few on your coffee table when guests come over, they will be impressed with how much you know about fishing.

Also, make sure that you are always carrying at least one fishing book or magazine around with you wherever you go. You can flip through it while on the subway, or while waiting for the oil in your car to get changed. This will make you look like a real fisherman because everyone else around you will be wasting their time reading newspapers or one of those celebrity gossip magazines.

You should also put a few of these books and magazines on your desk at work. This way, when coworkers come by, they will see these books and magazines on your desk and will know you are a great fisherman. And who knows? Maybe someday one of them will ask you about fishing. I like to imagine that someday, a coworker will come by my desk, see a big fishing book sitting there, and say, "Oh, you're a fisherman?" I will proudly respond, "Yep! I sure am. I am one of the greatest fishermen in the world."

I know I'm a great fisherman because I don't need any help fishing. I was out checking my pool for fish the other day (I still haven't had any show up), when my neighbor came out and asked if I ever wanted to go fishing with him. He told me some sad story about going fishing as a kid with his dad, and now that his dad was dead, he was looking for another fishing partner. He said he could show me some of his favorite spots, if I wanted.

I almost laughed at him, but was able to hold it in out of respect for his dead father. It was obvious what he really wanted. He saw how successful I had become, and wanted in on the action. So I said, "I appreciate the offer. I really do. But I honestly don't have time right now to show anybody else how to fish. I have the boat, the pool, the magazines, and all the best fishing gear. I even have the bumper stickers and t-shirts to prove how great of a fisherman I am.

"You don't have anything necessary for fishing, which shows you're not serious about it. I need to know you're serious and dedicated about fishing before I go fishing with you. If you want to become a fisherman like me, you need to start where I started and get a boat. I don't want to fish with someone who 'puts a hand to the plow and then looks back.'"

I could tell that last quote from the Bible confused him a little bit, especially since fishing and plowing have nothing in common. But he didn't argue. He knew he was out of his league and wasn't going to get any fishing secrets from me. So he turned away and walked back into house. It really was sad. But I had to say what I did. He would never make a good fisherman if he didn't make a commitment like I had. I was well on my way to becoming the world's best fisherman, and I couldn't have anyone slowing me down.

CHAPTER 11

FISHING RITES

To be a true fisherman, there are certain things you have to do which really don't make you a better fisherman, but prove to everyone else that you are the real deal, the genuine article. There are a lot of false fishermen out there, and the primary thing that sets true fishermen apart from false fishermen are fishing rituals. False fishermen don't practice these rituals, which prove they were never really fishermen in the first place.

I honestly don't understand the significance of these rituals, but I was told that true fishermen have been doing them for thousands of years, and so if I wanted to be a true fisherman, I would have to do them.

The first was net washing. I didn't own a fishing net, so I had to go buy one. I wasn't even sure how to fish with a net, but that didn't matter. Great fishermen of the past used these fishing nets, and so it was important to get one so that I followed the fishing tradition. But according to my reading, it wasn't just owning a net that was important, but cleaning it. So to identify myself with the great fishermen of the past, I began a daily practice of cleaning my fishing net.

I was determined to do a better job at it than others. For example, one guy on YouTube just sprinkled a little water on his net and called it good. It didn't take him more than a minute, and he said the water was just used for a symbolic washing anyway. But I doubt that fishermen of the past could clean their net in under a minute, and I don't think that sprinkling a net qualifies as washing. So I make sure to take more time on my daily net cleaning, and really get the net fully submerged under water.

Here is how I wash my net: First, I fill the tub with nice, hot water, and use some of my wife's bubble bath. Then I carefully immerse the net into the water, and massage it for about fifteen minutes. Next, I drain the water and rinse the net with some hair conditioner. Afterwards, I blow dry the net and hang it back up on the wall so it's ready for the next day. All in all, this daily ritual takes about 45 minutes. This might seem like quite a commitment, but properly washing your net is one of the first steps in becoming a genuine fisherman.

I also like to keep a log of how many net immersions I complete. Why? Because truly successful fishermen have completed thousands of immersions, and I wanted evidence of all the net immersions I have done.

The second ritual that fisherman must practice is actually made of three elements: Successful fishermen must eat, sleep, and breathe fishing. This is to prove that fishing is more than just claiming to be a fisherman; it's a way of life. Some fishermen are fishermen in name only, but true fishermen are fully committed to the way of fishing, and faithfully follow it for their entire lives. To prove this, they must eat, sleep, and breathe fishing.

To "eat fishing," I began to eat those little cheesy fish crackers. I love how each fish cracker has a little smile. This reminded me that being a fisherman was a life full of joy and contentment. I wasn't sure how many of these crackers I should eat, or how often, so for the first month, I ate one box per day. But I began to get sick of eating so many crackers, so I reduced my cracker eating to one box per week, then one box per month, and finally, I decided that all I needed to do is eat one cracker per month. To make it easy to remember, I started eating this cracker on the first Sunday of each month.

Somewhere during that first month when I was eating a box a day, I realized that fish couldn't live without water, and so the crackers by themselves were insufficient. Besides, the crackers made me *really* thirsty. So I started to drink water with my crackers. At first, I just drank tap water from my kitchen. Then I realized that fish don't actually live in tap water. They live in oceans, streams, lakes, and rivers. But I wasn't about to go down to any lakes or rivers to get water. Besides, if I drank that water, I might get sick. So I started to drink some water from my swimming pool. It still had some dead fish floating around in it, and the water tasted pretty bad, but these are the sacrifices one must make to be a true fisherman. At first, I drank as much water as I wanted to quench my thirst, but later, when I started eating only one fish cracker a month, I felt that all I needed to do was drink about a teaspoon of water.

To "sleep fishing," I bought bed sheets with fish on them. My wife said they looked like little boy sheets, but I told her that we were the only ones who saw them and it was important for me to take every step necessary to become a fully devoted fisherman, even if some of the steps seemed a little silly.

Learning to "breathe fishing" was the hardest thing of all. Fish have gills, and I'm pretty sure that if I tried to breathe underwater, I would drown. So until I figure out a way to breathe underwater like a fish, I decided that the best I could do was make sure that the air I breathe was fish-scented. But which scent should I use? There are many fish scents to choose from.

I started by leaving open cans of worms lying around the house, but my wife complained too much about the rotting worms all over the place, so the worms had to go. In their place I put some dead fish I pulled out of my swimming pool. But after a day or two, the house started stinking so bad my wife threatened to move out. She doesn't understand the great sacrifice of being a fisherman. Finally, I ended up leaving open cans of tuna lying around. My wife complained about this too, but I told her that I was making a tuna-fish sandwich, but had been interrupted in the process. She threw the cans out.

Then one day I was at the local pharmacy getting some Fisherman's Friend cough drops, and I saw a bottle of pills called "Cod Liver Oil." Each pill is a little gel-cap filled with cod liver oil. I bought a bottle and now every morning when I wake up, I take a cod liver oil gel-cap, poke a little hole in it with a needle, and then squirt it up my nose. It smells terrible, and I hack and gag for about twenty minutes afterward, but the smell of fish almost never leaves my nose. I am able to "breathe" fishing all day long. I know this sounds extreme, and probably only a few of us fisherman actually do it, but this just goes to show that the gate is narrow which leads to the life of fishing, and only a few find it. These fishing rites are the things you must do to prove you are a fully-devoted follower to the way of fishing.

CHAPTER 12

MEETING FISH NEEDS

I finally got around to reading the article in one of my fishing magazines about thinking like a fish. It said that if you want to catch fish you have to think like a fish. You have to understand what fish want, what they need, and what their goals are in life. If you can do this, you will catch more fish because you are meeting their needs. This is called "Need-Oriented Fishing."

The article pointed out that when businesses try to meet the needs of their customers, they learn what the needs are by doing surveys and opinion polls. Fisherman could do something similar with fish. But the article didn't tell me *how* to survey the fish. This is why these magazines are such a waste of time. They often tell you *what* to do without telling you *how*. This is probably because most of the authors were fake fisherman who never caught any fish. So I wracked my brain for weeks trying to figure out how to run a survey with fish, and I tried all sorts of experiments.

In one experiment, I wanted to find out if fish preferred grasshoppers or worms. Traditionally, worms are thought to be the common food of fish, but I heard somewhere that contemporary fish like grasshoppers because they are louder and more fast-paced. So I bought a bunch of worms and grasshoppers and dumped them in my swimming pool. I figured that whichever was eaten first would show me which one the fish preferred.

The only problem was that so far, even though I had previously put out signs and banners inviting fish to my pool, none had actually shown up. But then I realized what had happened. The fish had secretly visited my pool during the night and had eaten the flies and worms that were there from when I created the fish habitat with my neighbor's rocks and trees. After they ate all the flies and worms, they left. This meant I had to replenish the supply so that the fish would keep coming back. So I decided to regularly put worms and grasshoppers in the pool. Since this would meet the tangible needs of the fish, they would not only come and visit the pool, but maybe they would even stay.

One day, as I was trying to think of some other fish needs, I realized that to think like a fish, I had to start acting like a fish. But fish really don't do a whole lot. It seems like all they do is eat and swim. But if this is what I needed to do to think like a fish, then I decided I better get started. Maybe after I learn to eat and swim like a fish, I would be better equipped to understand the inner workings of the fish mind.

I began with eating like a fish. Since I believe that worms are the traditional food for fish, I resolved to eat a worm. I went down to the fishing store and bought a Styrofoam container of earthworms. When I got home, I asked my wife if she could cook the worms up in some sort of dish for dinner. She just laughed. I told her I wasn't joking, and she laughed harder. Women just don't understand fishing.

So I decided to eat a worm the old fashioned way, exactly like a fish: raw. I took a worm out of the container and held it up before my face. It was covered in wet dirt, and was squirming all over the place, as if it knew that I was about to eat it. I gagged a little just thinking about eating this dirty, slimy, squirming worm. And as I looked at it, I actually started to feel sad for the little guy. I cannot imagine it wanted to die a horrible death of getting crushed by my teeth, and then dissolving away in my stomach. The more I looked at this poor worm, the more convinced I became that eating a worm would be cruel. I am against cruelty to creation in all forms. So I threw the worms into the garbage can and sat down for dinner. My wife cooks the best veal.

But I still needed to eat like a fish. So the next day I went down to the fishing store again, and this time I bought some fake rubber worms. The clerk said these worked almost as well as real worms. I went home and tried eating one of these, but it was so rubbery I couldn't swallow it. I just chewed and chewed and chewed. I have no idea why fish like to eat these things. I eventually just had to spit it out.

I had struck out twice in trying to eat the same food fish eat. But I was a quick learner. I decided that although I should eat like a fish, I didn't like fish food, and so I needed to find something that was somewhat like fish food, but which a human could eat. Trying to eat the rubber worm had reminded me a bit of gummy worms, which I really enjoyed eating. I especially like the sweet and sour ones which are covered in sugar. So I went down to the candy store and bought a bag of assorted gummy worms. Then I ate the whole bag. Fish sure are lucky to be able to eat such food all the time!

After my success with eating worms, I decided to try swimming next. This really terrified me, because I hated water. I considered just going for a dip in my swimming pool, but since the water was terribly disgusting with all the dead fish from the pet store and the worms and grasshoppers I had thrown in there, I decided it would be better to swim in a natural body of water. Besides, there was obviously something wrong with my swimming pool, and I needed the real fish experience so I could learn how to get my pool to attract more fish.

But which natural body of water should I try to swim in? At first I thought about going back down to the river, but I knew that if I got into the river, I would be swept downstream and might die. So I went to the public swimming area at the local lake instead. The nice thing about this swimming hole is that a lifeguard is present. I knew that if something went wrong in the lake, I could always get rescued by the lifeguard.

As I drove down to the lake, I was a little nervous. It wasn't every day that one got naked in public. You see, fish don't wear clothes, and I knew that if I was going to experience swimming like a fish, I would have to swim naked. It would be embarrassing, but if you are going to become a serious fisherman, you have to be willing to make a fool of yourself. It's called being a "Fishing Freak."

Swimming like a fish in the lake did not go well. I had just gotten all my clothes off and was wading into the lake when people started screaming and yelling at me. Mothers frantically pulled their children from the water, and fathers yelled, "Get some clothes on!"

I was slowly wading into the lake because the water was so cold, and had only gone up to my knees when the lifeguard ran over and tackled me! We both went splashing into the frigid lake water. I bet no fish has ever been tackled by a lifeguard.

"I'm not drowning!" I yelled at the lifeguard. "I wasn't even up to my knees!"

"Pervert," said the lifeguard. "There are children around."

"Well, maybe they could learn a thing or two about fishing," I told him.

"You're going to learn a thing or two down at the county jail," he said. "The police are on their way."

"Police? But I have a fishing license," I said. "It's back on the shore. Want to see it?"

He didn't want to see the license, and a few minutes later the police arrived and took me down to jail. I got charged with public indecency in the presence of minors.

I thought about calling my wife to come post bail for me, but I knew she wouldn't understand. So I called my neighbor instead. He came and bailed me out, and then drove me back to the lake to get my car. We talked about a few stupid things like the weather, politics, and how his wife had a cancer scare, but he never once asked me about why I was in jail.

When he dropped me off near the swimming hole, he said, "Hey, before you go, I wanted you to know that the bail fee was $500."

"Wow. That's a lot." I said. "Fishing is *so* expensive. Well, thank you for helping cover some of my costs.

When I catch my first fish, I will have a plaque made for my wall which thanks you for your generosity."

He looked at me with a dull, blank stare as if he couldn't comprehend what I was saying. So I got out of his car and walked over to mine. I gave him a wave and a "thumbs up" sign as I drove off.

Through the whole experience I did learn why fish never come out of the water: they don't want to get tackled by lifeguards and taken to jail. This might explain why no fish have shown up at my swimming pool yet; they were too scared to come out of hiding.

So although swimming like a fish did not go nearly so well as eating like a fish, both experiences helped me accomplish my goal of learning to think like a fish. I learned that fish like sweet and sour candy, and that the reason they don't come out of the water is because they are scared of going to jail. Yes, I could feel my mind becoming more "fishy" every second.

CHAPTER 13

THE FISHING CHANNEL

There is only one thing better than fishing, and that is watching fishing on TV. In fact, I like watching fishing on TV so much, I have temporarily stopped fishing altogether. I feel so much more successful as a fisherman when I can watch others catch the "big one" and hear their tips and tricks for how they did it. Watching these shows reveals that if I was the one in that boat, with the knowledge that those fishermen have, I would be the one catching the big fish.

So while my wife thinks that watching fishing on TV is a waste of time, I think it is highly educational and encouraging. The things I learn about fishing will make me a highly successful, world-famous fisherman someday. I figure that the more I learn on TV, the better fisherman I will become. As a result, I turn on the TV first thing every morning to watch one or two fishing shows before work, and then I come straight home and watch fishing on TV for five or six hours every night.

My favorite fishing channel is the Trout Broadcasting Network, TBN for short. It has one fisherman after another, all day long, talking about how they almost got eaten by lions while fishing in Africa, the harrowing adventure they had while fishing in Communist China, and how the Taliban almost killed them when they went fishing in Iran. These TV fishermen almost never do any actual fishing on their shows, but instead share their fish tales in front of large audiences and crowds. It is very inspiring.

The fishermen on TBN are very successful. They are always surrounded by beautiful potted plants, golden furniture, crystal chandeliers, and brass statues of fish. One fisherman I saw even had a giant oil painting of a fish ascending into heaven from the lip of a waterfall. It looks like the fish jumped out of the water right at the top, and then just kept flying right up into heaven. It reminds me of how I sometimes want to leave this world behind and just fly up into fishing heaven where every backyard has a fully-stocked pool and where there aren't any annoying neighbors.

So I am always in awe when I watch these shows. I am not sure what fishermen paradise looks like, but it must be close to what they show on TV. Best of all, in all my hours of watching, I have yet to see any dangerous fishing rods or barbed hooks. There is never any water a person might drown in, and most importantly of all, these fishermen are so thoughtful of their viewing audience, they never show any stinking, rotting fish.

One of my favorite fishermen has his hair bleached out. He says it was sun bleached from all the time he spent outside fishing. He wears a fancy suit and gold rings, which are symbols of his success as a fisherman, and he has the biggest smile I have ever seen. I am always impressed at how white his teeth are! He also says that he never had anyone teach him how to fish, but God just miraculously gifted him with great fishing skill and knowledge. I wish God would do that with me.

Recently this fisherman personally asked me to participate with him in his worldwide fishing efforts! It was quite an honor. I was watching his show on TV, and in his signature shouting-cadence style, here is what he said:

> I AM-ah one of the world's greatest fisherMEN-ah of the world-ah.
>
> Can I hear an Amen? AMEN-ah! Glory be to God! Hallelujah! Praise Jesus. Praise HIM-ah.
>
> And I KNOW-ah that many of you would love to go fishing with ME-ah. And you can! Yes, you can! You CAN-ah!
>
> You want to know how-ah? Well, let me hear you say it today! Say, "Tell me how!" That's right-ah! Shout it

louder! SHOUT IT LOUDER! Amen-ah. Amen and Amen-ah.

Foom-cay-ta-la-toe. Azhim! Ey-lay-tay-eyana. Ah-la-a-za-ba-ta-la.

Do you want to go fishing with me?

Well, you can't-ah. You can't go fishing with me. It's too DANGEROUS-ah.

But because it is so DANGEROUS-ah, I cannot go ALONE-ah!

Say it with me! I CANNOT GO ALONE-ah.

Ah-la-a-za-ba-ta-la …

So I need your help-ah. When I go out into the world to rescue those poor fish-ah from behind their logs and deliver them-ah from their DARK holes, I need your HELP-ah!

Let me say it again: I NEED YOUR HELP-ah!

Here is what you can do.

You can support my fishing. You can partner with me in my FISHING! You can BECOME-ah my FISHING PARTNER-ah.

You see, it is expensive to fish, and the danger is great-ah, and the needs are many. The streams are WHITE with the HARVEST-ah of fish that need to be GLEANED-ah from within their swollen BANKS-ah, and I am willing-ah to go out into the RIVERS and LAKEBEDS-ah and call those fish to come in!

Say it with me, "FISH! Come in! Come on IN, FISH-ah!"

Our fishing efforts are short about $2 million this year. You say, "Why so much?" Because fishing is so EXPENSIVE-ah. That's why. Why is it so expensive? Because it's DANGEROUS-ah. It is DANGEROUS-ah!

Shout it out with me: "FISHING IS DANGEROUS-ah!"

That's why it is so expensive. It's expensive because it's dangerous.

But I am willing to take that risk, if you are willing to partner with me. If you want me to keep fishing these DANGEROUS waters, then I need your HELP-ah to keep my fishing GOING.

All you have to do is send in some money. If you send in whatever is in your wallet right now, I might be able to keep FISHING-ah for another DAY. If you send in whatever is in your checking account, I might be able to keep FISHING-ah for another MONTH-ah. And if you send in whatever is in your savings account, I might be able to keep FISHING-ah for another YEAR-ah!

The more you send in, the more you will be BLESSED-ah.

I remember back when I first wanted to be a fisherman, I helped support the fishing efforts of a different successful fisherman. I sent him every penny I had. And it hurt. I gave 'till it HURT-ah.

I said, "Ouch-ah!" when I gave.

Have you said, "Ouch!" recently? Maybe you SHOULD-ah.

Because after I said, "OUCH!" when I gave to that other fisherman so many years ago, I got so BLESSED-ah. And look at me now! My donation to that other fisherman has increased TEN-fold, a HUNDRED-fold, even a THOUSAND-FOLD-ah!

And that can happen to you! It can happen to YOU!

Amen. AMEN. AMEN-ah. Say Amen.

La-sa-da-ba. Ay-ya-la-yo-nee. Ya-she-na-ash-lo-so-nee-mah. She-lee me-dah-nah ...

You want to become a successful fisherman like me? You need to say, "Ouch-ah!" So take out that checkbook, pick up that phone, and send in a donation-ah. And don't just give 'till it hurts. Give 'till you say "OUCH-ah!"

Say it with me, "I want to say, 'OUCH-ah!'"

Yes, that's right. And let me give you that opportunity right now-ah.

Tonight only, if you support my FISHING efforts with your GENEROUS donation-ah, if you send in a donation of $100 or more-ah, I will send you a crystal jar filled with water from my favorite fishing hole. I caught the BIGGEST fish-ah of my life-ah out of that hole-ah, and with this jar on your shelf-ah, you are guaranteed to catch BIGGER fish more often than ever BEFORE-ah!

Don't miss out! Call in today and support my worldwide fishing efforts! The number is on the bottom of your screen, and operators are standing by waiting for your call.

Now let us pray.

After I heard this offer, I called in right away and made a donation of $1000. My wife and I had several bills due in the next couple days, and giving this money meant that we would not be able to pay our bills. But since I wanted to become a world-famous fisherman, I knew that I needed a bottle of that fishing water. Besides, by supporting this other fisherman in his work, I was partnering with him in his fishing. In a way, by giving money to him, I became his fishing partner. Every time he caught a fish, it would be as if I was right there catching fish with him.

I was well on my way to becoming a world-famous fisherman, just like the man on TV!

CHAPTER 14

ATTENDING THE FISHING CLUB

I wore my fishing shirt to the mall today. As I checked out, the clerk behind the counter noticed my shirt and said he was a fisherman too! It's amazing where you run into other fellow fishermen.

"Where do you attend a fishing club?" he asked.

I actually had never heard of a fishing club before, but didn't want to appear stupid, so I mumbled something about how I am still looking for a good one.

"Oh! Well you should visit mine this week! We gather on Sunday mornings and talk about all the best fishing spots and techniques. Sometimes we hear stories about great fishing trips of the past, and every once in a while, someone shares their favorite fishing technique or gives away their secret fishing hole. It would be a great way for you to fellowship with other fishermen!"

So I went. The meeting started at 10:30 AM on Sunday morning. The group met in a big, beautiful building, and when I walked in, a guy greeted me at the door and handed me a little pamphlet which explained what the group was going to do that morning.

The meeting began a little oddly though. Someone got up and led us all in some fishing songs. I have never been much of a singer, but I did find myself tapping my toes along to a few of the songs. One of them almost brought me to tears when we sang about the suffering of a kingfisher.

After we sang, another guy got up and he asked if there were any newcomers that day. I tried to huddle down into my seat so no one would notice me, but the guy who invited me raised his hand and pointed to me.

"We got one here!" he shouted.

"Well, stand on up, brother!" the man up front said.

Everybody cheered and clapped, and someone gave me a "Welcome Packet" which had useful information about what their club was all about and why I should become a full-fledged member. There was even a gift-certificate for a free copy of the fishing club leader's newest book, *Your Best Fishing Now!* It sounded good. I would definitely pick up my free copy at the Welcome Center in back after the meeting.

After I was welcomed, another man stood up front and spoke for about half an hour from their Fishing Manual. He began with a story of a one-armed fisher-man who miraculously got his second arm back so he could cast his nets on the other side of the boat. The story gave me goosebumps. Then he went on to tell us that emotionally and psychologically, all of us are one-armed fishermen, and if we follow three simple steps, we can get our arms back. This was really helpful information and explained a lot about why I was having trouble fishing. He said that in order to get our missing arm back, we have to stay true to our word, honor our promises, and keep committed to fishing, and especially to the fishing club. I almost stood up and clapped, but nobody else did, so I stayed in my seat.

After the teaching, they passed around little brass plates. Surprisingly, as the plates went from person to person, people dropped money into them! As the plate got closer to me, I took out my wallet, thinking that I had to put some money in the plate, but the man who invited me whispered that I didn't have to give anything since this was my first time. He later explained that these were their fishing dues, and all faithful and committed members of the fishing club are expected to put 10% of their income into the plate.

After the meeting, we stood around drinking coffee and I was able to talk to many other fishermen about their favorite places to fish. It turns out that not very many people in the club actually do any fishing. They just tell stories about friends of theirs who heard about a guy who caught dozens of fish on a stretch of a river in Africa, or another guy who pulled a fish so big out of a frozen pond in Minnesota that the fisherman had to make the hole in the ice bigger just to pull it out.

All the stories were very inspiring. Prior to attending this fishing club, I was feeling bad about not having caught any fish. I was beginning to wonder if I was *ever* going to catch a fish. But now that I met a whole bunch of other fishermen who had also never caught any fish, but who knew lots of amazing stories from people who had, it made me realize that this is just the way it is in fishing. Some people go fishing; others tell inspiring stories about fishing.

I really became encouraged after talking to one white-haired old-timer.

"How long have you been attending this fishing club?" I asked him.

"I've attended faithfully for 57 years. I missed one meeting back in 1973 when I caught pneumonia, but the club leader called me up to make sure I hadn't abandoned fishing, and it was so encouraging to know that he cared about me so much that I haven't missed a meeting since. I love coming every week to hear about the fish people are catching."

"Do you have any great stories about the fish you've caught?"

"I have never actually caught a fish," he said. "But as one of the great fishermen of the past said, 'One baits the hook, another casts the line, and a third reels in the fish.' I see my role as a baiter. Of course, I don't actually bait any hooks either. That's too dangerous."

I nodded my head. I had already learned about the dangers of fishing hooks.

"I generously and joyfully support the work of other fishermen," the old man went on. "I help them buy the bait."

"Oh. So you don't actually buy the bait either?" I was intrigued about this because although I had only been a fisherman for a short time, I had already bought some bait. It sounded like this old fisherman hadn't even done that.

"Never!" he laughed. "You have to go through four years of specialized training in order to know what kind of bait to buy. I was never able to get that training. And of course, the ones who buy the bait don't actually bait the hooks. You have to get more training for that. A third person has to be trained to cast the baited hooks into the water, and a fourth person is specially trained to reel in any fish that are caught. Fishing is a whole process and one person can't do it all by himself."

This was a real revelation for me, and explained why I was having so much trouble: I had been trying to fish all by myself! But now I saw that fishing takes a whole community of trained specialists. I now saw how foolish I had been to go buy bait on my own, or to even dream of catching fish without some specialized training.

It was also obvious that I was going to have to start regularly attending this fishing club. I told this to the man who brought me, and he beamed ear-to-ear as we went over to inform the fishing club leader of my decision.

"This is great news!" he said. "I have a six-week class that starts next week. If you want to become a fishing club member, you will have to attend the entire class. At the end of the class, you will have to sign our membership agreement and our fishing creed, start giving 10% of your income to the club as membership dues, and you will also have to get immersed into the fishing fellowship."

"Immersed?" I asked. "I'm not all that fond of water."

"Well, it is the first step in becoming a fully devoted follower of the fishing lifestyle. If you don't get immersed, you cannot be a fisherman. But don't worry, we use a bathtub filled with warm water. It's just like taking a bath at home, only much quicker."

"Do I have to be naked? I got arrested a while back for public nudity."

"We all make mistakes in life," the man assured me. "Now that you're going to get immersed, your entire life will never be the same. But to answer your question, no, you won't be naked. We give you a clean, white robe to wear. It represents how pure and pristine your new life as a fisherman will be."

That sounded just great, and I told him so.

"I might also have some difficulty with giving 10% of my income," I told him. "My wife has been spending a lot of money recently." Truth be told, our financial problems were my fault, because of all the fishing gear I had purchased recently and that big donation I had made to the TV fisherman. But my wife bought some new shoes recently which I didn't think she needed, so I could blame her.

"There is a high cost to fishing," the leader said. "Other fishing clubs hold to cheap fishing, but we believe in putting all the requirements on the table right from the beginning so that people know that fishing is costly. If you are not willing to pay the cost, then you might want to examine yourself to see whether or not you want to get in the boat."

I told him that I had already bought a boat, and the most expensive fishing gear for my boat, and even installed a swimming pool for the boat. I knew full well about the cost of fishing. Who was he to question my commitment to fishing?

He was clearly impressed at how much I had spent on fishing. He went on to say that in cases like mine, the fishing club could temporarily waive the 10% fishing dues requirement if I gave my fishing boat and most of my fishing equipment to the club in lieu of my fishing dues. If I donated my fishing gear, they would waive my fishing dues for one year. He went on to explain that as a fishing club member, I could still use the gear as often as I wanted; it just wouldn't belong to me.

He told me a story about a fishing club from two-thousand years ago who had all their fishing equipment in common, so that no one had any needs. That is what this modern fishing club wanted to do too, but they needed generous donors like me to give all my stuff to the club so that it could be available to all.

This sounded like a good deal, and I took him up on it. One year of no fishing dues will give me some time to start paying off the loans for the boat and the pool. Also, my wife will be amazed at my generosity when I tell her I gave the boat, the pool, and most of my fishing rods away for free.

Immediately that afternoon, after lunch and a nap, I started draining my pool while loading up my fishing poles into the back of my truck. As I was doing this, my neighbor sauntered out of his house. He saw what I was doing and came over to investigate.

"So you're 'throwing in the towel'?"

What an idiot. Isn't it obvious what I'm doing? "No." I told him. "Do you see any towels? I'm draining my pool and loading up my fishing gear."

"Right. What I mean is, are you giving up on fishing? Are you quitting?"

"Of course not! This is the next step in becoming a fisherman. I'm donating all my equipment to the local fishing club. I attended today, and they said that if I donated all my stuff, I wouldn't have to pay dues for a whole year."

"Hmm. A fishing club, huh?" He grimaced while he said it. "You know, I used to attend a fishing club."

I stopped dead in my tracks and turned my head to look at him in surprise. "You used to attend a fishing club? Does that mean you used to be a fisherman? This is the first time you've ever said anything about it."

"Well, I'm still interested in fishing. I just don't go about it the same way you do. I also don't attend a fishing club anymore. I found it got in the way of actual fishing."

"Oh." I continued to walk back toward my truck with the armload of fishing gear. "Well, then you probably aren't much of a fisherman. I learned today that all true fishermen regularly attend a fishing club."

"I wouldn't say that," he cautiously replied. "A lot of the guys at the club don't even fish, you know."

"Yes, they told me today. But that's because fishing is not a one-man job. One person needs to bait the hook, another needs to cast the line, and the third needs to reel in the fish." It felt good to quote some of what I had learned at the fishing club that morning.

"Right. That's what they told me too. Well, look … I know you're sort of just getting started on this whole fishing thing, but can I suggest that you hold on to most of your fishing gear for a bit longer? That club … they have enough fishing gear already. Some of what they get they just sell for the money, but most of it sits in an empty lot behind their building."

Now that he mentioned it, I *had* seen a bunch of junk behind the fishing club building after the meeting today. I didn't want to think that my boat and poles would end up there. Maybe this was the smartest thing my neighbor had ever said.

"All that junk fishing gear is because some people donate junk." I said. "My stuff isn't junk. It's top of the line. So they won't junk it or sell it. They'll use it to catch the biggest fish the world has ever seen."

He looked doubtful. "Maybe," he said. "But just take a night and think about it, okay? I would hate for you to have spent all your money on that great fishing gear just to give it all away to a group that doesn't really need it."

"I'll keep the boat," I said. This was mainly because I don't know how to get it loaded back into my boat trailer, but he didn't need to know that. "But I gave my word on the rest, and so I'll be taking it over there first thing tomorrow morning. I am a man of my word and I keep my promises." I hadn't actually given my word, but my neighbor was making good sense and I didn't want him to get puffed up with pride by me telling him.

Late that night, after my neighbor had gone to bed, I unloaded all the fishing gear into my garage and then shut the garage door so he wouldn't see it. I wanted him to think I had actually donated it, and that I was fully committed to my fishing club. Just because he was a backslider from the club didn't mean that I would become one.

My wife complained about not being able to park her car in the garage, but I told her that these were the sacrifices we needed to make for the fishing club. "The club always comes before family and marriage. I need to be fully committed and a man of my word," I told her. She said I had made a promise to her before I had picked up this foolish fishing hobby, and so I had to choose between the hobby and her.

Her ultimatum made me pretty upset, but I have to admit that she made a good point. It is definitely important to honor my commitments, keep my promises, and stay true to my word, just as they taught me at the fishing club.

I sure do hate sleeping on the couch out in the garage with my fishing gear. But during my first night on the couch, I turned on the radio since I couldn't watch the Fishing Channel. The very first song I heard was "I'm Gonna Miss Her" by Brad Paisley. This was a clear sign I had made the right choice.

CHAPTER 15

LEARNING THE LINGO

Fishermen are not as smart as they once were. Over the past fifty years, fishermen have been "dumbing down." I blame the television. I used to watch a lot of television, but I don't watch as much as I used to and I can feel myself getting smarter every day. Everyone should stop watching television just like me. Of course, since I'm sleeping on the couch in the garage, I couldn't watch television even if I wanted to.

Anyway, to counteract this increasing ignorance, it is critical for a fisherman to learn to talk like a fisherman. True fishermen know all the big fisherman words, and can casually throw fishing lingo into any conversation. After I started attending the fishing club every week, I quickly learned how little I knew about fishing.

During the weekly fishing lectures, and in conversations with other members after the meetings, I found myself in awe over all the big fishing terms people threw around which I did not know. There was talk about dispenfishionalism, fishcatology, angler awareness, covenants of fishing, efishiency quotient, the hydrostatic union, filioquota, and numerous other terms I didn't understand.

It wasn't just the lingo. There were debates about which types of hooks were approved by God, how old a person could be before they went fishing, whether or not women could fish, and whether or not fishing could be done with rubber worms. Clearly, I had much to learn.

So the next day I went down to the local fishing bookstore and asked for some books on systematic fishology. The clerk led me over to an isle filled with hundreds of giant volumes.

"Is there a particular book you're looking for?" he asked.

I panicked. If I didn't sound smart, he would know that I was an amateur fisherman who was just trying to learn the lingo. So I blurted out a line I had heard someone say at the fishing club the previous Sunday.

"Yes, I want to learn about pneumatological participatory martyrological fishcatology." I had no clue what this meant, but apparently he didn't either, because he turned to scan the rows of books, while stroking his chin and trying to look smart. Finally, he pulled a few books from the shelves and handed them to me. They were some of the smaller volumes, and most of them were in paperback.

"I think these are a little too basic for me," I said. I couldn't understand the title on most of the books, but that didn't matter. I wanted him to know that I was serious about learning my fishing lingo. I pointed to a set of books near the end of the row which had boring brown covers. There must have been ten or fifteen books in the set, and they had the word "Dogmatics" on the spine.

"How about those?" I asked. "I don't own a fishing dog, but I am going to get one, and I think that set would be helpful in training him to fish."

The bookstore employee just laughed. I had no idea what he was laughing about, so I laughed too. I picked up one of the volumes and thumbed through it. The print was incredibly small and looked terribly dull. I really had no plans of getting a fishing dog. I wasn't even sure that dogs could fish. But apparently it could be done, and based on the length of the set, training a dog to fish must be quite difficult to do.

"Yep, this is the set for me," I said, and loaded it into my cart.

On the way up to the check-out counter, I noticed an isle filled with colorful fishing statues, some fancy fishing pens, and even some small vials of "Miraculous Fishing Oil." I grabbed several of each item. Those fishing pens would come in handy when I recorded the number and size of all the fish I caught. And I wasn't sure what miraculous fishing oil would do, but it sounded like a good way to catch more fish. At the check-out counter, there were some refrigerator fishing magnets and some fishing greeting cards. I bought several of these too.

When I got home, I put the magnets on my refrigerator, the pens, cards, and oil on my counter, and the statues and books on my shelf. Wow, they looked nice! Very impressive.

I decided right then and there to send a fishing gift basket to my neighbor. I included a round container of "Filamints" that looked just like a spool of fishing line, a fish-shaped cookie cutter, a set of chocolate hooks, a live-action fishing computer game, and a set of brightly painted fish figurines. I also included a card with some nice fishing slogans inside. At the bottom of the card, I signed my name and said "Sure would love to have you join me at the fishing club this Sunday!"

The other members of the club sure would love it if I brought my neighbor on Sunday. I had been telling them a lot about how rude and ignorant he is, but it would show that I was a really great fisherman if I was willing to introduce him to the fishing club.

When I saw him next, he thanked me for the basket, but didn't say he would come to my fishing club. He is so ungrateful! I told my fishing group what had happened, and one man said it was because my neighbor was "totally deprived" of fishing. Another guy agreed, and said that the eyes of my neighbor's heart were darkened. I don't know how a heart can have eyes, but I nodded anyway. Best of all, I was learning some great phrases that I could start using in other conversations. The more fishing lingo I learned, the better fisherman I would become.

CHAPTER 16

THE FISHING TRAINING CONFERENCE

Recently at my fishing club it was announced that a Fishing Training Conference was coming to town, and everybody who wanted some intensive preparation in being a fisherman should register to attend. There were several big-name fishermen who were going to speak, and the fishing club leader said that he had been going to this conference for years and benefitted from it every time. He also encouraged us to register early. If we paid at the door for the three-day conference, it would cost $249 to get in, but if we registered early, the cost was only $239. That sounded like a good deal to me, so I called up that very day and paid.

I was still in debt financially from giving $1000 to the TV fisherman, and my wife had made me promise that I would not buy any more fishing gear until we were out of debt. But this wasn't fishing gear. It was a conference fee. In fact, the more I thought about it, it wasn't even a fee. It was an investment in my future fishing efforts.

On the first day of the conference I pulled up to the conference center, full of excitement and anticipation about what I was going to learn. But I immediately felt out of place. I had worn jeans and a fishing t-shirt, but most of the people going into the conference were wearing fishing waders, fishing vests, and fishing hats. A few even carried fishing poles. Initially, I felt ashamed that I had not dressed more appropriately, but then some of these impressively-dressed fishermen started talking to me, and my shame turned into awe. I couldn't believe that I was hanging out with such dedicated fishermen! When I imagined having fishing friends, this is what I imagined. It was thrilling to hang out at a conference and talk with other men who knew how to dress like a fisherman. On the second and third day of the conference I made sure to dress to the hilt in all my fishing gear. I even put a little mud on my boots to make it look like I had just come from the river.

The first thing I did at the conference was visit the registration table. A nice man behind the counter helped me check in. His shirt said, "I've Been Fishing with Cheeses." I didn't know fish liked cheese, but decided not to show my ignorance by asking him about it. The man found my name on the list of pre-registered attendees and gave me a nametag. The nametag had a blue sticker on it, which indicated I had preregistered. He said that people who did not preregister did not get a blue sticker. He also said that the conference speakers had been given red stickers. I looked around and saw that only about half of the attendees had blue stickers. It made me feel good to be in the "Blue Sticker" group.

The worker then gave me a conference schedule and invited me to go browse the wide selection of fishing books which had been written by those who were going to speak. I went excitedly over to the books to see what was available, and before I knew it, had five or six books I planned to purchase. One of them was called *Lifestyle Fishing* and another was *Conversational Fishing*. Both seemed to be focused on the idea that fishing was a natural event that could happen as I went about my daily routine. This sounded very nice, as the more I learned about fishing, the more burdensome it became.

I was looking through a book called *Discovering and Using your Gift of Fishing* when a man came up next to me.

"That's a great book!" he exclaimed.

I was just about to say that it looked good to me too, when I noticed his nametag. He did not have any stickers. Not even a blue sticker like mine. How much could this guy know about fishing if he didn't even preregister?

"Ha!" I laughed. "This guy doesn't have anything to say I didn't already know. I know so much about fishing, I could have been a speaker at this conference. The only reason I have a blue sticker instead of a red one is because I decided to take a break from speaking this year. We fishing experts need to be humble enough to let others do some instruction now and then. One of these days, you might know enough about fishing to know this is a terrible book! In fact, see this author?" I pointed to the picture of the author on the back. "He knows nothing about fishing!" I slammed the book down to emphasize my point.

The guy looked at me shamefacedly. It was good that he recognized a better fisherman when he saw one. As he turned and walked away in a dejected manner, I quickly picked the book back up and put it on top of the pile of books I was planning on buying. As I did so, someone else spoke on the other side of me.

"That's a great book!" he said.

"No, it isn't!" I responded. "It's a book for beginners. I'm buying it for my five-year old son at home."

As I said this, I turned to the man who had just spoken. He had a red sticker. His face looked vaguely familiar too.

"A book for beginners, huh?" he asked. "Well, I'm the author of that book, and while I agree that it's a book for beginners, we're all beginners at one time or another and I suspect that it might do you some good to read it."

I looked at the name on his nametag. Sure enough, he was the author of this book.

"Well, uh, you know … I didn't mean … all I meant was …" I had to think quickly. "When I said it was a book for beginners, I meant that I really enjoyed reading this book when I was a beginner, and I think every beginning fisherman should read it. But now that I am not a beginner, I am ready to move on to more advanced material, such as the books about *Fishing Dogmatics*." Thankfully, I remembered the name of the set of books I had bought recently at the Fishing bookstore.

"Oh! You've read the *Dogmatics*?" he asked. "What did you think of the author's idea that the fishing covenant is the presupposition for reconciliation between landowners and fishing trespassers?"

"Ha! Wouldn't you like to know!" I said. "I am preparing a lecture on that very topic to present at this fishing training conference next year. If I tell you what I think, you'll just steal my ideas." And with that, I turned around and walked away. I really had no clue what he was talking about, but as long as I gave the impression of knowing, that was all that mattered.

Over the course of the three days, I heard some great speakers and attended some fantastic workshops. One of the first speakers taught us about "Lifestyle Fishing." He said that most people think that fishing is just something you do on the weekends, or whenever you feel like it. As a result, such people are poor fishermen and never catch any fish. To be truly successful, you have to practice "Lifestyle Fishing" which is where everything you do is geared toward fishing. When you go eat breakfast at the local diner, you should ask the waitress if there are any food scraps around that could be used as fishing bait.

He said that fishing should always be on your mind and you should always be looking for "divine opportunities to fish." You can even take fishing breaks at work if there is a pond on the property, or maybe a fish tank in the lobby. The speaker said that if your boss objects to you fishing at work, you should say that your fishing rights are protected by the Constitution, that fishing employees are happy employees, and all bosses should want happy employees.

I did object a little when he said that we should have it as our goal to get to know our neighbors so they could become fishermen too. The speaker clearly doesn't know my neighbor, and if he did, I doubt he would have said that. My neighbor is impossible to deal with.

Another speaker talked about "Conversational Fishing." He gave us some fantastic tips and tricks for injecting fishing subjects into almost any conversation. If someone was talking about the weather, we could say, "Yes, the sunshine today sure is nice. I wish I could be fishing." If the conversation was about politics, we could say, "The only reason politicians argue so much is because they don't go fishing." If the conversation was about a war in another country, we should say, "If more people in that country went fishing, they wouldn't have wars."

I took many pages of notes on this topic, and plan to inject the subject of fishing into almost every conversation from now on. Also, this seminar proved to me once and for all that my neighbor knew nothing about fishing. Though he had hinted a time or two that he used to fish, he never tried to inject fishing topics into our conversations. I was the one who did that, which proves I was the true fisherman and he was not.

One of the seminars I went to was about "Discovering and Using your Gift of Fishing." The man presenting the seminar handed out a test with 100 multiple-choice questions on it. When the tests were scored, we learned which of us had a special skill for fishing and which ones did not. I actually scored pretty low on the test, and was quite upset for a minute or two. But the presenter assured us all that if we scored low, it doesn't mean that we weren't meant to be fishermen. He said that everybody is supposed to be a fisherman, but for some it just comes more naturally. For the rest of us, we will have to work at it and learn how to fish more successfully, which we could do by attending conferences like this one. This made me feel much better.

One of my favorite sessions was called "The Way of the Master Fisherman." It was co-taught by some guy I had never heard of and a famous Hollywood movie star who was more famous as a child. They said that most fish thought they were good fish, but our job was to convince them that they were bad fish. Once we had done that, we were to convince them that they could become good fish if they jumped into our boat. The approach sounded kind of mean to me, but the presenters assured us that this was the way a Master Fisherman of the past had caught all his fish.

Another great session was on "Fishing Explosion" which uses a Question and Answer survey to ask fish about their behaviors and beliefs. Most fish don't have time to answer the questions, and the instructor informed us that you may have to ask the same questions to hundreds—even thousands—of fish before you get one to answer. He said it works best if you write the questions on sticks of explosives, and toss them into a river or lake. The fish that come to the surface are the ones who want to hear more. Using this approach, you are guaranteed to catch fish, even though the ones you catch are somewhat pulverized from the explosives.

Finally, I liked the session about "How to Plan a Fishing Crusade." The idea here was to gather a huge school of fish all into one place, and then through the use of emotional music and persuasive fishing techniques, get a few of them to come into your fishing net. It sounded very expensive.

I did pick up some new lingo as well. I heard many speakers talk about choosing the proper "Fishing Targets" and how to "Seal the Deal" with fish who are "on the fence." I also found it highly instructive to learn that there are only two kinds of people in the world: Fishermen and Pre-Fishermen. That explained a lot to me, since I always wondered why some people seem to have no interest in fishing. I now knew that one day they too would see the light and become a fisherman like me.

I can't wait until the Fishing Training Conference next year. They already announced two of the speakers. One is from Houston, and will be speaking about "Your Best Fishing Now" and the other one from California has agreed to present the topic of "Purpose Driven Fishing."

On the last day of the conference, they told us that while we waited for next year's conference, we could buy the CDs of all the talks from this year, and listen to them all year long. We could even share the CDs with others as a way to invite them to next year's conference. There were twenty CDs for $97, so I bought a set and added them to the box of fishing books in the back seat of my car.

If my wife finds out and asks me why I bought all these fishing books and CDs after I promised not to spend any more money on fishing, I'll just tell her that they're all for my neighbor, who needs to be introduced to the joys of fishing. Maybe after he listens to these CDs and reads these books, he'll come to the conference next year.

CHAPTER 17

THE FISHING PRAYER

At the Fishing Training Conference, I heard one speaker say that the key to catching fish is to faithfully pray the fishing prayer. He taught a whole seminar on the history of the fishing prayer and the amazing catches of fish that some fishermen had experienced after praying this prayer. The prayer is written in an archaic style, so he even went through the prayer line-by-line and word-by-word to teach us what it meant.

Here is the Fishing Prayer:

Our Father above the water,
Hallowed be thy name.
Thy rain will come, thy rivers run,
On earth as they do in heaven.
Give us this day our daily fish,
And forgive us our excess limit,
As we forgive those who set the limit.
Lead us not into rough water;
Deliver us at the end of the season.

For Thine is the river, the ocean, and the fishing glo-
ry

Forever and ever, Amen.

The man recommended that we pray this prayer at
least once a day, but he said that those fishermen who
had the most success prayed it at least three times a day.
So I memorized the prayer and began to recite it at every meal. I even went the extra mile and started reciting it
in the morning when I woke up and at night before bed.
Since I am praying it five times a day, I am almost guaranteed to become the greatest fisherman the world has
ever seen. I am sure that by this time next year, when
the man gets up to teach all the amateur fisherman who
have never caught a fish about the miracle-working
wonders of this prayer, he will have some stories to tell
them about me, and how I prayed *five* times a day, and
as a result, caught the biggest fish in the world and the
most fish ever in one day.

Just dreaming about how great of a fisherman I was
going to become made me want to tell my neighbor.
But I realized I couldn't just go tell him that I was a
great fisherman. I had to show him. So I decided to start
saying the early morning fisherman prayer out in my
fishing boat. I got up just before dawn and went outside
and climbed into the bow of the boat. Then, with my

arms raised to the Great Fishing Father in the sky, I shouted the prayer at the top of my voice.

The problem is that the prayer is kind of short. I got all the way through it, and I don't think my neighbor even heard me say it. So I decided to pray it again, even louder this time. But he still didn't appear. I ended up praying that prayer eight times before he finally came outside. His hair was a mess, and he was only wearing boxer shorts and a t-shirt. He clearly had no sense of shame.

He looked at me quizzically, and then looked up into the sky.

"What's all the shouting about?" he said, rudely interrupting my prayer. "My wife and I were trying to sleep, and you woke us up."

"I was praying, of course," I responded scornfully. "What kind of heathen doesn't recognize prayer when he hears it? Praying early in the morning is one reason I am the greatest fisherman in the world. I pray five times a day."

"I don't know if shouting a prayer over and over at dawn makes you the greatest fisherman in the world, but it certainly makes you the worst neighbor. If you keep this up, I am going to have to call the cops. I started working the late shift down at the factory, and I cannot be woken up at dawn by your shouting."

I am always amazed at how rude my neighbor is. But it reminded me of what one of the other speakers at the fishing training conference had said, about how we would get ridiculed, mocked, and persecuted for being a fisherman. He even said that we might even make our wives and kids hate us, but that is part of the cost of being a fisherman. But still, I didn't really want my neighbor to call the cops.

"Fine," I said. "I'll pray a little quieter from now on. But you really shouldn't be sleeping this late in the day, anyway. The early bird gets the worm, you know."

To be honest, I had trouble getting up that early in the morning anyway, and was never able to do it regularly. But I did make sure that every time my neighbor was out in his lawn or driveway during the daytime, I got up into my boat and raised my arms to heaven and shouted my prayer once or twice to the fishing father. I wanted to remind my neighbor that I was the greatest fisherman in the world, and though he may infringe on my right to pray early in the morning, he couldn't stop me from praying during the day.

One of these days, after seeing my fervent prayers, he might actually become a fisherman also, and I could teach him all my tips and tricks.

CHAPTER 18

STRATEGIC HELP IN TRAINING PEOPLE TO LOVE ANGLING NOW

Along with the Fishing Prayer, another thing I learned at the Fishing Training Conference was the importance of writing up a document called the "Strategic Help In Training People to Love Angling Now" (SHITPLAN for short).

The speaker quoted a great verse out of the Bible which said, "People perish for lack of fishing." One of our goals as fishermen, he said, was not to do all the fishing ourselves, but to teach others to fish as well. Then he quoted that famous proverb (which is probably from the book of Proverbs): "Give a man a fish, feed him for a day; teach a man to fish, feed him for a lifetime." He said that he had plaques for sale in the conference bookstore with this saying on it. They cost only $59.99. I bought two, one for my office and one for my car.

The speaker went on to say that people perish because they don't know how to fish, and so if we teach them to fish, they will not perish. But the problem is that most people don't want to fish, and so it was up to us to take them fishing with us when we go.

I raised my hand and said that in the past, I had tried to invite people to go fishing with me, but nobody wanted to go. Of course, I didn't mention that I hadn't actually been fishing yet either, but the speaker didn't need to know that.

The speaker must have liked my question, because he spent the next ten minutes answering it. He first said that people will join us if they know where we are going. He said that you can tell if you are a leader or not by looking behind you to see if anyone is following. I was sitting in the front row, and when I looked behind me, I saw the whole room of people. I was definitely a leader in the world of fishing.

Then he went on to explain how we can tell people where we are going. We have to develop a plan called the "Strategic Help In Training People to Love Angling Now." He explained that this plan would include a list of values and goals for my life as a fisherman, as well as my mission, vision, and purpose statements. I wasn't exactly sure what all these things meant or how to come up with them, but thankfully, the speaker said he had written several books on these topics, and they could be purchased at the conference bookstore. I bought two copies of this book as well, just in case I lost one somewhere.

Hearing what this speaker had to say answered a lot of questions for me. Up until now, I had always wondered why I hadn't attracted any fish into my fishing pool, why I didn't have the courage to go fishing on a lake or a river, and why nobody ever joined me on my Fishin' Mission. Now I knew that before I could make progress in my goal of becoming the world's greatest fisherman, I needed to write my "Strategic Help In Training People to Love Angling Now" document.

Preparing this plan would probably take months, but if this is what it takes to be a world-famous fisherman, I couldn't waste any time. Actually going to fish would have to wait until my SHITPLAN was written.

Researching and writing my SHITPLAN took so long, I wasn't able to go outside to my fishing boat, or say my prayers in the bow. My neighbor came over a few times to check on me and see if I was okay and needed anything. He said he wanted to make sure I wasn't sick. He is *so* nosy. I bet he only wanted to check in on me because he wanted to steal some more of my fishing ideas.

One time he even said that I needed to get outside more, and offered to take me fishing with him. I laughed and told him that I couldn't go fishing until I finished my SHITPLAN, since it was the key to making sure I fished in the right area, used the right bait, for the right type of fish. He looked at me a little strangely, and asked me what a SHITPLAN was. I tried to explain it, but it's hard to explain these things to a non-fisherman.

When I was done, he said, "You know, you don't really need any of that to be a fisherman. All you have to do is go spend some time down on the water, throw in a line, and see what happens. I can help you do this if you want."

I laughed. "If you don't think I need a SHITPLAN to fish, then you can't teach me anything about fishing," I said. "In order to properly fish, you have to know your values and mission and purpose and goals, and you have to put this all down on paper so that you can print it up and distribute it to others, so that when you become a world-famous fisherman, you can show others how to follow in your footsteps and do what you did. If you want to teach others how to fish, then you need to know what you've been taught. But if you don't know what you've been taught, then you can't teach others, and therefore you can't fish. It's perfectly logical."

He just shook his head and said, "Well, I don't have any strategic plan to help others love fishing. But if you ever want to give up the planning and just start fishing, let me know, because I'd love to take you with me."

I thanked him for his kind offer, but then rolled my eyes as he walked away. How could he possibly fish if he didn't have a SHITPLAN? But I was writing mine, which meant I was going to become a world-famous fisherman.

It took me a couple more months of research, planning, writing, and rewriting, but I finally came up with a 46 page document which contained my mission statement, vision statement, purpose statement, values, and goals. I even included a bunch of the fishing lingo I had heard at the fishing club and learned from my fishing books. Then I printed a hundred copies down at the copy shop and showed one to my wife. She tried to read it but couldn't make sense of the first paragraph. I guess that's just because she's not a fisherman.

CHAPTER 19

FISHING IN AFRICA

Recently at my fishing club, we had a special presentation from a fisherman who had just come back from fishing in Africa. He said that fish there were so hungry, they would bite on anything! He went on to tell some miraculous stories about how he got special permission to fish in some tribal fishing waters, and how the biggest fish he caught was out of a little stream of water in central Ethiopia. He also showed many pictures from various African Safaris he had been on so that he could take pictures of lions and zebras. I don't know what this had to do with fishing, but it sure made Africa look dangerous.

His presentation got me thinking that to become a world-famous fisherman, I needed to do two things. First, I needed to actually go fish somewhere in the world. Africa would be great! Second, since I was having so much trouble catching fish here in the United States, maybe it would be easier to go to Africa where the fish were hungry and the streams weren't so fished out. Here in America, all the fish know all the tricks of fishermen. Fish have seen and heard it all before. But if I went to Africa, I could catch boatloads of fish every day!

That afternoon, after I got home from the fishing club, I announced this plan to my wife.

"How are you going to pay for it?" she asked. That's my wife, always putting a damper on things because of money.

"The value of one fish is worth all the gold and silver in the world," I responded. "What is a little expense to bring fish into the creel?"

"That may be true," said my wife. "But you're going to need some of that gold and silver to buy yourself a plane ticket to Africa. After all the money you've spent on fishing so far, we're broke."

She had a point. The bank had been sending me letters about some missed mortgage payments.

But it didn't take long for my crushing intellect to discern a solution. After the fisherman from Africa had spoken in our fishing club on Sunday, the club leader told us that we all should consider financially supporting the work of this fisherman in Africa. We could become a "donor" and receive special "Supporter Updates" from the fisherman about where he was going and what fish he was catching.

We were also told that the fisherman needed to build a 5000 square foot fishing hut in Africa so that he could rest after his exhausting fishing trips, and purchase a top-of-the-line Toyota Land Cruiser to safely travel on the bumpy dirt roads. I was amazed at the sacrifices he was willing to make, especially since the average African family lived in less than 500 square feet, and walked pretty much everywhere they went. Just imagine! We had the privilege of helping this man buy his house and car in this rugged African wilderness.

I didn't have any money to give, but it made me wonder why I couldn't do the same thing. Why couldn't I raise support and send out fundraising letters? My wife may be right that *we* didn't have the money to send me to Africa, but I knew that where God guides, God provides. I believed God was guiding me to Africa, and so He would provide for my needs to get me there.

It was really quite easy. I wrote up an impassioned letter about the poor fish in Africa, and how I was going to go over to them and help clean their water, give them food, and make sure the tribal warlords didn't bring fish to extinction. Furthermore, I was also going to help the poor and needy people of Africa. Some fishermen only give one fish to the poor so they can eat for a day; I was going to teach them to fish so they could eat for a lifetime. Springs of living water were going to appear in the dry and dusty desert of the Sahara. I also promised to bring back an expensive souvenir from Africa for anyone who gave me a donation of $100 or more.

The money poured in. Before long, I had more than enough to send myself on a six-week fishing trip to Africa.

When I arrived in Africa, at the edge of the Sahara desert, my first shock was to discover that there was very little water anywhere. This was going to be a problem. How could I fish if there was no water? How could I teach anyone to fish if there was no water? What kind of report could I bring back to my supporters at home if I told them I just spent six weeks looking for water, but was unable to find any?

I needed a backup plan.

The first thing I did was send out another support letter. I revealed in the letter that the situation in Africa was more dire than I had ever imagined. They had no water, and where there is no water, there is no fish. And if there were no fish, I could not teach anyone to fish. So we urgently needed more money—fast! I also told people to pray for rain.

Once again, the money poured in. The first thing we did with the money is build a giant above-ground swimming pool. It was pretty much just like the one I had back at my house, but much bigger. And since we had so much money to spend, we made this pool even fancier. We surrounded it with imported marble, lined it with gold trim, and erected a giant stained-glass fishing pole reaching up into the sky.

But there was still no water. The support team from back home must not be praying for rain hard enough. So I sent out a third support letter, full of pictures and images of the beautiful swimming pool we had built for the hungry and starving people of Africa. I impressed upon my supporters that before I could teach the Africans how to fish, we needed to fill the pool with water. And we were only going to use the best water for our African fishing hole swimming pool. We were going to import millions of bottles of Perrier sparkling water and dump them into our swimming pool. The people of Africa drank really disgusting water and there was no way we were going to put that in our swimming pool.

Just as before, the money poured in. We bought the Perrier and dumped it into the swimming pool. It was beautiful. The water sparkled in the desert sun and it looked like the perfect place to go fishing. So I announced to the poor people of Africa that fishing lessons would begin the very next day.

"How are we going to catch fish in a swimming pool if there are no fish?" asked one old man.

I laughed at him.

"That just shows how little you know about fishing!" It truly is amazing how backward and ignorant people are in third-world countries. "I know from my vast experience as an expert fisherman that before you can catch any fish, you must first learn *how* to fish. And that is what I will begin teaching tomorrow."

But the next day when we all met at the swimming pool, it was empty! At first I accused them all of stealing the water during the night, but upon further investigation we discovered that the pool had sprung a leak and all the water had poured out into the desert sands. I blame the faulty African construction methods for this mistake. It was quite a disappointment for us all.

Thankfully, my flight back to the United States was the next day. I told the Africans to fix the leak and get more water, and then I would be back to teach them how to fish.

Upon my return to the United States, I went around to many fishing clubs praising them for their support of my fishing efforts in Africa, and telling them of the great success we had there. I gave many slide-show presentations. Somehow, I neglected to take any pictures of the drained swimming pool, and so that particular tragedy never made it into my otherwise glowing report.

CHAPTER 20

WORLD FISHING TRAINING CENTER

It turns out that going to Africa was the best thing I ever did for my fishing career. That trip is what finally launched me onto the path of becoming a world-famous fisherman. Something about traveling across the ocean and helping African people made it seem to others that I truly was a great fisherman. Even though I had never really caught a fish here in the United States (or even in Africa), people just assumed that I must be a great fisherman because of my dedication and service overseas.

So after I got home from Africa, some of my donors suggested that I start a "Training Center" for fishermen. There were numerous fishermen around the country and across the world who were dying to know all that I had learned about fishing, so that they too could become successful fishermen.

This training center would have all the best books and equipment. It would be a safe place where fishermen could come for training. We would not only teach the fishermen trainees everything they needed to know about fishing, but would put them in real-life scenarios where they could practice the skills of fishing, without any danger of drowning, getting pierced by hooks, or getting arrested for swimming. At our school, they could become master fishermen without any contact with smelly fish.

The first thing I had to do was start an advertising campaign. I needed brochures and billboards, television spots and radio ads. And on every single one, I had to put a picture of myself.

So I had a professional photographer come over to my house. I put on my best fishing t-shirt and my golden fishing necklace, and had him take pictures of me standing in front of all my fishing books. For a special touch, he told me to open a leather-bound fishing book and point my finger at some random place on the page to make it look like I was studying it.

When I got the proofs back, I was quite impressed. With my fishing clothes on, all those fishing books behind me, and the open fishing book in my hands, I really looked like a world-class fisherman. Everybody would want to learn from me now!

Then I had a graphic design artist put together a little brochure with my picture on it, which included my mission, vision, values, and purpose statements from the SHITPLAN I had written previously. I included a description of my dream for a World Fishing Training Center, and how the only thing that was keeping us back from transforming the world into a fishing utopia was a lack of finances.

Then I sent this brochure out to everybody who had financially supported me on my fishing trip to Africa, and I sent it to every fishing club I could think of. When the donations started coming in, we hired a realtor and an architect so we could buy land and construct a giant building upon it. We eventually found a piece of property on the north side of town. It was 80 acres and only cost about half a million dollars. I know this sounds expensive, but we needed lots of room for parking.

Then we had the architect draw us up some plans, and as soon as they were done, we began construction. I learned from my experience in Africa that people are impressed with beauty, and so we decided to use only the best building materials. We built our training center with marble flooring, brass handrails going up spiraling staircases, giant stained-glass windows which depicted famous fishing scenes, two huge LED screens, and a state-of-the-art sound system. Altogether, the first stage of construction was estimated to be about $10 million, and we had future plans for additions and renovations that could cost upwards of $150 million with a 90,000 square foot auditorium that seats 3000 people.

We would also construct several dormitory-style buildings, complete with padded seating, fold-out tables, and electronic whiteboards to start a four-year intensive training school for young fishermen. We would hire some of the best fishermen from around the world to come and pass on their knowledge to the next generation.

Yes, with a training center like this, we were certain to turn the world upside down. It was just a matter of time before we caught every fish in the world.

At one point during our fundraising efforts, I went and knocked on my neighbor's front door to ask if he wanted to donate any money. I told him that if he gave enough, we could even put him on the board. He sadly shook his head and said that he didn't think it was a wise use of money to spend millions of dollars on a fishing training center. He asked if maybe the money could be better spent to feed the hungry or provide housing to the poor.

I laughed at his ignorance. "First of all," I said, "the poor will always be with us, so we will never be able to solve the problem of poverty. Second, the poor are only poor because they won't go get a job. Third, it's training centers like this one that will actually help the poor. We will be able to bring hundreds of fishermen here a year to train them how to fish, and when they all start catching fish, there will be too much fish for them to eat, and they will use the extra to feed the poor."

Then I told him about the little old lady down the street who had given me the last two hundred dollars from her bank account. "It's not about the amount you give," I said, "but the spirit in which you give it. She didn't have much, but she gave her all. It was very touching to see. But you can't give anything? That's very selfish of you."

He looked upset. "Are you talking about Mrs. Miter? The widow? You know she lost her husband last year, and she's living on a very meager fixed income. And you took her last two hundred dollars? For what? So you could buy a couple bricks for your training center? That was probably her food money for the month. What is wrong with you?"

"There's nothing wrong with me," I said. "It's just that I believe in miracles, and you don't. I told Mrs. Miter the story of a great fisherman of the past who turned five loaves of bread and two fish into enough food to feed thousands of people, and when they had all eaten their fill, there were twelve baskets of food left over. I told her that if she gave us her last two hundred dollars, God could give her two *thousand* dollars in return, or maybe baskets and baskets full of food … more than she could ever eat!"

He looked at me in disgust and then slammed his front door in my face. So I turned around and went home and sat in my living room to read a fishing book. A few minutes later, through my living room window, I saw my neighbor come out of his house. He was carrying several bags of groceries, and as I watched, he took them down to Mrs. Miter's house.

I almost started weeping. I couldn't believe how quickly God had miraculously provided for her needs, just like I had promised! This was going to be the perfect story to include in my next fundraising letter. Then the money would *really* start pouring in.

CHAPTER 21

THE FISHING COVENANT

After I started the World Fishing Training Center, I had thousands of students who came and went through the courses we offered. But I soon began receiving reports that after the students went back to their homes, few of them were actually doing any fishing. It made me question what we were doing and why. If the students we trained to fish never actually did any fishing, there a problem with our training or there was a problem with the students.

Upon reflection, I determined that it was the student's fault. Most of them were not truly committed fishermen. Though they seemed like true fishermen at the beginning, the fact that they fell away and never actually fished proved that they were never fishermen to begin with. They were spurious fishermen.

Somehow I needed to develop a way to determine true fishermen from false fishermen. I could not have any fishermen who put their hand to the rod, and then later turned away. I needed a lifelong commitment to fishing. So I sat down and put together a fishing covenant. It was a document which provided the seven proper beliefs and ten proper behaviors of all true fishermen. If a potential fisherman trainee could not agree to this fishing covenant, then they were rejected from my training center and were counseled to examine themselves to see whether or not they were a true fisherman.

Below is the fishing covenant I developed:

I, (Your Name Here), commit to uphold the beliefs and behaviors of all true fishermen as outlined below, proving thereby that I am a fisherman in truth.

Seven Proper Fisherman Beliefs

1. The Fisherman's Guidebook is without error, and is the only source for proper fisherman beliefs and behaviors.
2. People who do not fish are living without hope and without purpose in this world. It is our job as fishermen to convince others to become fishermen also.
3. The Great Master Fisherman of the past is our prime example for how to be fishermen today. We must follow his life and actions as closely as possible.

4. The Great Master Fisherman will return in the future to inaugurate an era of peaceful fishing upon the entire world.

5. There have been seven periods of fishing throughout human history, each with distinct rules and ways of fishing. We must not confuse the rules of our era of fishing with the rules of other eras as this would lead to faulty forms of fishing in the present time.

6. The Spirit of Fishing is at work throughout the entire world to draw men to fishing. We are agents of this Spirit when we live lives in accordance with the beliefs and behaviors explained herein.

7. Women are not allowed to be fishermen. We are called "fisher*men*" for a reason, even if we don't know what that reason is.

Ten Proper Fisherman Behaviors

1. Fishermen will regularly attend an established fishing club where they will receive instruction and training about the ways of fishing. The truly committed will attend Sunday morning, Sunday night, Wednesday night, and Saturday morning.

2. Fishermen will give 10% of their income to the fishing club they attend.

3. Fishermen must read and study the Fisherman's Guidebook for at least fifteen minutes every day.

4. Fishermen must not allow their hair to grow past their collar. Fishermen are to be disciplined, and a high and tight haircut reflects an orderly and disciplined life and mind.

5. Fishermen must not exaggerate about the number and size of fish they catch. Honesty and integrity are the hallmarks of all true fishermen.

6. Fishermen must not use coarse language when fishing, but should only allow pure and encouraging words to escape their lips.

7. Fishermen must not drink beer when fishing. Beer is of the devil.

8. When a fisherman catches a big, beautiful fish, the fisherman must not dance. Dancing is undignified and may lead to sexually explicit behaviors.

9. Fishermen must only purchase fishing equipment (such as fishing lures and fishing boats) and fishing materials (such as books and magazines) from other fishermen who are due-paying members of their own fishing club. We want to keep our business "within the family."

10. Fishermen must only listen to fishing music. Other types of music may lead fishermen into

behaviors which are not proper for true fishermen.

Signed,
(Your Signature Here)

As an added benefit to this fishing covenant, we now have a way to silence all the critics of our fishing methods. If someone criticizes what we teach or how we train, we can just see whether or not they have signed the fishing covenant. If they have not, then we denounce them for being false and lying fishermen, and we seek to warn others not to listen or heed anything these false fishermen say.

One final nice thing about this fishing covenant is that I made sure to leave out all references to actually catching fish. As my experience has shown, fish are notoriously difficult to catch, and it would not be right or fair to require true fishermen to catch fish. Although I did indeed want the graduates of my Fishing Training Center to catch fish, I knew that in time, they would naturally start catching fish if they took the first step of signing my fishing covenant. When fishermen are first starting out on the path of fishing, it is enough for fishermen to move toward fishing, think about fishing, and invest their money in the lives of others who do fish, or with people like me who train others how to fish.

After I wrote up the fishing covenant, I took it to my board of directors for approval. Jim and David refused to sign it. This shocked me because these two men were some of my closest friends on the board and they had probably caught more fish than the rest of us combined. I asked them why they refused to sign the Covenant. Jim said he liked to have a beer every now and then with his fishing buddies and didn't see anything wrong with it. David said that he and his wife liked to go down to the local dance hall on Friday nights, and he believed that this weekly date had kept their marriage together.

I really did hate to have to vote them off the board. But I can't have false fishermen on my board of directors. It was probably their presence on the board that was part of the explanation for why so few graduates of my training center were not actually catching fish. But now that we had cleaned house, things were sure to change.

Due to the shocking departure of Jim and David, the board also agreed to add an eleventh point to the fishing covenant list of behaviors. We believed that Jim and David had become polluted by the non-fishing world because they hung out with people who didn't fish. So we added this eleventh standard:

11. All true fishermen will only befriend and spend time with other true fishermen who have also signed this fishing covenant.

After the board meeting, I had the fishing covenant engraved on brass plaques and gave one to each board member who had signed it. I also took one over to my neighbor. As he was reading through it, I mentioned that two board members had refused to sign it, and so we had voted them off the board.

"Yeah, they told me," he said.

"What?! Are they spreading gossip, lies, and rumors about me and the training center board? Now I know it was the right thing to remove them. When did they tell you?"

"Jim and David are two of my closest fishing buddies. They introduced me to fishing many, many years ago. And they just told me that you voted them off the board. That's true, isn't it?"

I scowled at him. "Well, yes. But they probably didn't tell you the whole truth about why they got voted off the board. We wouldn't do such a thing without very good reasons."

He raised his eyebrows when I said that. "Are you implying that they had some sort of moral failure or that they lied about fishing? I don't know anybody on that board who does that." I sensed some sarcasm in his voice, but he was still talking so I didn't ask him what he meant. "All I know is that Jim and David are two of the greatest fishermen the world has ever seen, and they taught me everything I know. Your training center board is now much weaker than before."

He handed the brass plaque back to me. "I don't want or need this," he said. "Jim and David are meeting me later today down at the river to see what we can catch. You're welcome to join us if you want."

"I can't," I said. "I signed the covenant and I am not allowed to hang out with false fishermen like you guys."

CHAPTER 22

JOE THE FISHERMAN

It had been a while since I had last talked with my neighbor … probably a year or two. It's not that I was trying to ignore him. I had been busy with going to Africa, starting my World Fishing Training Center, and reading fishing books. But as I sat in my living room one day, thinking about whether I should accept an invitation to speak at a fishing conference, my mind began to wander to my neighbor.

I felt a little bad that although I was a world-renowned fisherman, I had still not been able to convince my neighbor to become interested in fishing too. Though I had invited him to my fishing club multiple times and had given him lots of fishing literature, he had never seemed interested in any of it. Although he had hinted a time or two that he liked to fish, I knew he wasn't a real fisherman because I never saw him do any of the things that I did as a fisherman.

Yet something was definitely going on with him, because over the past year or so, I had seen many people come and go from his house. Sometimes he had eight or ten people over there all at once. At one point I thought maybe he was a drug dealer, but after I called the cops, they assured me that he wasn't. So now I just assumed that the constant visitors at his house meant that he had trouble keeping friends. After all, he had been so rude to me over the years, I wasn't surprised that he couldn't maintain a relationship.

What was *really* strange was that my wife often went over to his house as well. I hadn't been able to ask her about it because I had been so busy with all of my training activities for fishing. But as my mind wandered to thinking about my neighbor, I realized that I could use my wife as leverage to get to him. If I worked it right, I bet I could get her to ask him to come to my fishing club this Sunday.

I decided to start by taking her on a date. I actually couldn't remember the last time we had been on a date, so I knew she would love it. Besides, she had been a little distant and cold lately, so I knew that a date would help our marriage.

I went all out. I remembered that she liked the food from a Mexican grill downtown, which we had last eaten at before I became a fisherman. I decided to take her there. Then I stopped by the local grocery store to get her a bouquet of her favorite flowers.

But when she got home from work and I gave her the flowers and announced that we were going on a date, she got this crazy look in her eyes like I was insane.

"That Mexican grill closed down three years ago, and it was never my favorite place. It was *your* favorite place. I liked going there because I liked being with you. And lilies are not my favorite flowers. They are the flowers you use to decorate your fishing club. I hate them. In fact, I'm allergic to lilies."

I tried to interject that we only decorated with lilies during a special time of year in the spring, but she wasn't finished.

"And besides," she said, "you can't expect me to get home from work at 5:00 and be free for a date at 5:30. I have plans tonight. Furthermore, why would I want to go on a date with you tonight when you couldn't even remember our anniversary three days ago?"

This helped explain her strange behavior that day. I had been to meetings all day with my fishing club buddies, and when I got home, there were lit candles all over the house, my favorite dinner was on the table, and my wife was wearing a skimpy dress. When I asked her if the electricity and air-conditioning had gone out, she coldly responded that the spark was definitely gone. I could tell she wasn't in the mood for conversation, so I took my dinner and ate it in my study, but that only seemed to make things worse. Now I understood why.

"Well, you should have reminded me a day or two before," I responded. "And besides, I didn't really forget; I'm just *postponing* it until we can celebrate it properly. I've been doing a lot of studying and teaching for the fishing club and the training center, and I have to set priorities. After all, as a famous fisherman once said, 'Anyone who desires to be a fisherman, but does not hate father, mother, wife and children, brothers and sisters, yes, his their own life, such a person cannot be a fisherman.'"

"So it's *my* fault?" She was starting to get a bit shrill. I hate it when she does that. "And rather than apologize and say that you do love me, you instead say that you hate me? What is wrong with you?"

I decided that it probably wasn't wise to correct her. I hadn't said that I hated *her*. I had only quoted a great fisherman. It is so annoying when people misunderstand and misquote the greatest fisherman of all time this way. But I had to let this pass so I could figure out why she was so angry. After all, the only reason I asked her on a date in the first place was because I was hoping she could help me get over to my neighbor's house so I could invite him to the fishing club.

"Honey muffin," I said. (She *loves* being called food names. At least ... I *think* she does.) "I am *sooo* sorry that you don't like lilies and can't understand the pressure I'm going through at the training center. And I'm sorry the Mexican restaurant closed down. It must have been a big blow to you since we have so many good memories there." My only memory of the place is the really good burrito, but I'm sure my wife has memories of our conversations there. Women remember those sorts of things. "But look, I'd love to spend some time with you and try to make it up to you. Where are you going tonight? Can I tag along?"

"Sure, if you want to." She seemed a little surprised and even pleased that I would want to join her in one of her activities. I hoped it wasn't something boring like clothe shopping or taking a walk through the park. "I'm getting together with a bunch of people for dinner, and then afterward we're going to plan how to help that family down the street who are going through some hard times …"

She went on to explain more about this needy family, but I wasn't listening. I was desperately trying to think of a way to get out of this. The last thing I wanted to do was help a needy family on our street. I had enough problems of my own.

"… so Joe will love seeing you and will be thrilled to learn that you are joining us tonight."

"Wait … Joe?" I didn't know anybody named Joe. "Who's Joe?"

She looked at me like I was crazy. "You know … Joe! Our neighbor? Are you serious? We've been living next to him for years, and you've have dozens of conversations with him, but you never even learned his name?"

Whoa! I thought to myself. *My neighbor is going to be at this meeting tonight! This is what I was trying to accomplish anyway, and the opportunity just fell into my lap. There is no way I am going to miss this. And best of all, I've just learned his name, which will make it that much easier to act friendly and personal around him.* "Oh! Joe! I call him Joseph. I didn't know he was going to be there. I'd love to go!"

"Alright, well, we're nearly late, so let me grab my cake and let's go." She went and took a beautiful cake from the refrigerator and then headed toward the front door.

"Did you make that cake?" I asked. "When did you learn to decorate cakes?"

She sighed and shook her head. "I've been taking classes for the past year. It's where I met some of the people who will be at Joe's tonight. Last month in one of the classes …"

I didn't hear anything else she said. My mind was already thinking about how I would convince Joe to join my fishing club. I had thought that the date with my wife would be just the first step in getting her to invite me over to my neighbor's house, and here I was, thirty minutes later, walking over to his house with her! My plan had really worked out well. The fishing gods were really smiling down on me tonight!

CHAPTER 23

THE FISHING CHARADE

It turned out I wasn't the only fisherman headed for Joe's that night. As we walked up his driveway, I counted four trucks with fishing gear in them. If I wanted Joe to come to my fishing club, I was going to have to work fast, as others were apparently trying to recruit him too.

As my wife introduced me to the people, I couldn't believe how much she knew about them and their lives. She knew their names and where they worked, and even asked a few people about their children. But what shocked me more is that several of the people knew all about *me*! They greeted me by name and one person even asked about my fishing training center. *My wife must really be proud of me to tell others about everything I have done,* I thought.

While we walked around and made small talk with people about stupid events in their life, I couldn't help but overhear several discussions among others about fishing topics. What is more, most of them weren't talking about the books they read or the conferences they had attended, but the actual fish they had caught. It even sounded like some of the women had gone fishing.

I was just about to interject myself into one of these conversations to warn them about the dangers of fishing and to say that no woman should ever be allowed to fish, when I was halted by a smell so amazing, I could hardly think straight. I looked around to see where this smell was coming from, and saw that Joe had just opened the door from his back yard where he was holding a platter heaped high with some sort of grilled food.

"The fish is ready!" he hollered. "Come and get it!"

I followed my wife out to the back patio and saw several tables lined with plates and cups, and one table in the middle had seven huge serving trays filled will all kinds of cooked fish. There was baked fish, grilled fish, fried fish, and some sort of fish, rice, and vegetable stew I didn't recognize.

As I walked up to the table with my eyes bulging and my stomach growling at the delicious smells, I noticed that each platter had a tent card in front of it explaining what kind of fish it was and how the fish was prepared. There was grilled garlic butter rainbow trout, breaded and fried largemouth bass, and a baked lake trout labeled "Firecracker Fish." It was made with crushed peanuts, green olives, sundried tomatoes, and some spices. The description said that each bite exploded with a mouthful of texture and flavor. It looked incredible.

As people gathered around, Joe thanked everyone for coming, and then briefly explained where each fish had been caught, who had caught it, and what fishing technique they had used. I noticed that three of the dishes had been caught by Joe himself at locations that were right outside of town.

It was then that I knew this was all fake. No true fisherman would ever give up his secret fishing holes or fishing strategies. This entire night must be a joke or a hoax to make fun of me, the world's greatest fisherman. These fish had probably been catered by some fancy restaurant. Worst of all, my wife was somehow in on this, trying to make me look foolish in front of her friends. Maybe this was her way of getting back at me for postponing our anniversary without telling her.

I decided to confront Joe about this. After how great of a neighbor I had been to him, this was how he repaid me? By lying to me in public, and trying to use me as a joke? But as I angrily stalked toward him, I noticed a large board off to one side filled with photographs. I moved closer to inspect it. Many of the pictures showed Joe standing on the shore of a lake or river holding a fishing pole in one hand and a large fish in the other. Several pictures contained other people as well, whom I recognized as other dinner guests.

As I was examining the pictures, my wife came up behind me. She was carrying a plate piled high with fish and handed it to me. It smelled delicious. As I took a bite, I almost choked at how good it tasted. I had never eaten anything so amazing in my entire life.

"Pretty tasty, huh?" my wife asked.

"It's okay," I answered, as I stuffed another forkful into my mouth. "So who are all these people and why do the pictures make it look like they fish?"

"They don't 'make it' look like they fish. They *do* fish. They caught and cooked all the fish on the table tonight. And they're all friends of Joe. He taught every single one of them how to fish. He invited me to join him at one of these dinners a while back, and I've even been going fishing with his wife a few times a month. See? There's a picture of us there." She pointed at a picture on the board which showed her and Joe's wife standing in the bow of a boat proudly holding up a giant Northern pike with huge teeth. "That's what you're eating now. I caught that fish. Do you like it?"

I stared at my plate. Then I stared at her. Then I looked again at the picture. I couldn't make sense of it. If this was all a hoax, it was the most elaborate and mean joke anyone had ever played on me.

But before I could say anything, my wife continued talking. "I've been trying to get you to come meet these people for over two years. I know how important fishing is to you, and I knew that these people could help you actually start fishing. Just like they've helped me. If you want to fish, you can join any one of them at any time."

As I struggled with shock and confusion at what I was seeing and hearing, a hand on my shoulder startled me back to awareness. It was Joe.

"Hey! It's so good to have you here tonight! Your wife finally pulled you away from work, huh? Have you had any more mishaps with your hooks lately?" He chuckled at his remark, but I knew it was an insult.

"I don't know what's going on here, but this whole fishing charade has got to stop. And to think that you dragged my wife into this! None of you know anything about fishing, and even if these pictures are real, and all your stories from earlier are real, none of you have the proper training or experience to go fishing. It's danger-ous to just go out and fish. I'm the one who attends the fishing club. I'm the one who started the fishing train-ing center. I'm the one who's read all the best fishing magazines. I bet you don't even have a good fishing pole. What pole did you use to catch this fish?" I point-ed at one of the pictures on the board which showed him holding a 26-inch brown trout.

He looked closely at the picture. "Hmm … I don't actually know. I think it's just some pole I got down at Walmart a few years back. It's nothing fancy, but it clearly did the job."

"See? And where do you keep your fishing boat?"

"I don't have one."

"What? Then whose boat is in this picture of my wife catching a pike?"

"Oh, that boat belongs to Kristin. She lets anyone borrow her boat who wants to." He motioned to a woman sitting at a table on the other side of the yard. She apparently was telling a fishing story to a rapt audience at her table. Their eyes were wide in wonder as she motioned with her hand about how large the fish was that she caught. She was clearly exaggerating, as a woman would not be able to catch a fish that large.

"But you don't have your own fishing boat?" I pressed. "How can you call yourself a fisherman if you don't even have your own fishing boat?"

"I just go fishing. Sometimes I borrow Kristin's boat, but usually I just fish from shore. Or a dock if there is one. Sometimes I wade into the water up to my waist to get a little deeper out."

"You actually wade into the water? And you get wet? Don't you get cold?"

"Sometimes. That picture of the 26-inch brown trout was taken after wading through a Montana river for about an hour. When that picture was taken, I couldn't feel my toes. But it was worth it. Look at that beautiful fish!"

"You were in the water with that fish? Weren't you afraid it would bite you?"

"Bite me? The fish?" He laughed. "No, I can't say that's ever been a fear of mine. Although now that you mention it, I think I might have had a fish nibble on my toe once at Tally Lake. It startled me, but no harm was done. I was standing in about a foot of water, so the fish probably wasn't that big. I suppose it could have been a crawdad that pinched me though … I didn't actually see what it was."

I didn't know what to say. Meeting someone who had actually caught fish was so rare, and Joe's backyard seemed to be filled with such people. "So, uh … what are your favorite fishing magazines?"

He shrugged his shoulders. "I don't really read magazines. I might've read one or two several years back, but I've always found that the best way to fish is just to get on the water and see what you can hook."

"Don't get me started on hooking," I said. "The last time I tried it, my wife told me it was illegal and just about divorced me."

He looked at me strangely, but didn't press for more details. "So … what do you think about going fishing with me and some of the guys tomorrow? We've got this little trip planned to a beautiful stretch of river outside of town. We'd love to have you come along."

It was then that I realized what this entire night was all about. "Oh! Now I see! You all are 'wannabe' fishermen, and you thought that if you could get me to go fishing with you, then you all might learn some secret fishing tricks or discover my secret fishing holes. You see how famous I have become, and you want to become famous too. Well, too bad, so sad! I hate to burst your bubble, but becoming a world-famous fisherman takes years of dedication, study, and hard work! So don't think you can take me fishing with you one time and become a great fisherman like me!"

He looked thoroughly confused. "Uhh … no," he said. "We actually thought you'd like to see one of our favorite fishing spots, and learn a few of our favorite fishing techniques. And maybe even catch a fish or two. Then we could come back here and cook them up like some of the fish you've eaten tonight. And remember Jim and David from your board of directors? They're going to be there too. Maybe you guys could patch things up and become friends again."

"Ha! *Now* it's all clear to me. You're jealous of my career as a famous fisherman, and you're trying to ruin my reputation! I can't hang out with Jim and David. They used to be true fisherman, but they went out from us, showing that they didn't really belong to us. If I fellowship with them while fishing, I might lose my job too. So get behind me! I'm done with your whole fishing charade."

With that, I turned on my heels and headed back toward my own house. But before I went, I filled up my plate again with some of the fish from the table. It looked like there was plenty to spare, and there was no sense in having it go to waste.

CHAPTER 24

BECOMING A PUBLISHED FISHERMAN

Some of my detractors have begun saying that even though I taught Africans how to fish and founded the World Fishing Training Center, I was not a successful fisherman because I had never actually caught any fish. And though he never actually came out and said it, I feel like my neighbor was one of those critics.

To show them how wrong they are, and to demonstrate to my neighbor that I was indeed an excellent fisherman, I decided to write a book. There is nothing better than writing a book for establishing credibility and proving that you are an authority in your area of expertise. After all, the word "author" is in "authority." I had spent so much money buying books about fishing, attending fishing conferences, going to Africa to fish, and founding the World Fishing Training Center that although it was true that I had never caught any fish, this did not make me any less of an expert in fishing. And a book would prove it.

I initially wanted to write a book called *Red Fish, Blue Fish* as a way of talking about different types of fishing by Democrats and Republicans, but my agent told me that someone had already written a book with that title. I went down to the library and read this book. It was mostly pictures. And these pictures were not very well drawn. I bet the author has never even caught a fish, or even sold any of his books. But since the title was already taken, I couldn't use *Red Fish, Blue Fish* as a title. Besides, I don't know a whole lot about politics, and my agent told me to focus on my area of expertise—fishing.

So I wrote this book instead, the book you are now reading. This book proves that I am a great fisherman, possibly the greatest fisherman the world has ever seen. This will be especially true if this book becomes a Wall Street Journal and New York Times best seller.

And look! You're reading this book right now! Doesn't that prove that I am a great fisherman? Of course it does! If I wasn't a good fisherman, why would I write a book about it? Why would anyone read it? The fact that you are reading this book about fishing proves that I am a great fisherman.

Another nice thing about being a published author is that it gets you invited to speak at conferences, which increases your visibility and platform in the fishing world, which then allows you to get more books published. This becomes a never-ending cycle of publishing and speaking which can become a great career! Who knows? If I am successful enough, maybe I can even start my own line of t-shirts and bumper stickers to sell at these training conferences. This will *really* prove that I am a world-class fisherman.

After this book was published, I decided to take a hundred copies over to my neighbor's house. I knew he would want to give them away to all his friends and tell them that he knew the author. I even signed the copies. I wrote, "If you ever want to *really* learn how to fish, come join me at the fishing club! Hope to see you there!" Then I included the address and telephone number of the club underneath.

As I was unloading all the boxes of books onto his front porch, Joe opened the door. "What's all this, then?" he asked.

"I wrote a book on fishing," I said. "And I know that you would really benefit from reading it. It not only contains all the greatest tips and advice on fishing, but also the secret locations and best equipment to help you catch more fish. You've been trying to learn all my secrets for years ... well, here they are. The book also has some pretty funny stories, just to spice things up. You're in several of those stories."

"I am? Well, it will be interesting to see what you wrote about me. I guess I'll give it a read." He didn't sound very enthused. "The invitation is still open to go fishing with me sometime. Have you caught a fish yet?"

"Nope. But I've realized that catching fish is not the only goal of fishing. Fishing is primarily about teaching others to fish. That's what this book is about. I know all the best strategies and methods, and I pass them on to others in this book, who will hopefully teach others also."

"But don't you think you need to actually catch fish before you teach others to fish?"

"Only ignorant and untrained fishermen think that," I answered. "Some people 'do,' while others 'teach.' I am one of those who teaches. If you read my book, you'll see. Besides, you can't really fish until you've read a bunch of books about fishing. You really need to start reading more if you ever want to become a fisherman like me."

He raised his eyebrows and smiled a bit. "I do okay. I tend to think that the best way to learn how to fish is to just go fishing. You make a lot of mistakes that way, but half the fun of fishing is learning from your mistakes."

I laughed. "That right there is why you're not a world-famous fisherman. Truly great fishermen never make any mistakes when they fish. Why not? Because they studied to prepare themselves to be a fisherman who doesn't need to be ashamed of what's in their tackle box or how they cast their line over the water so that it doesn't return to them empty. It can take years and years of studying before a true fisherman actually goes out to catch fish. But when he does, he catches more fish and bigger fish than anyone else. That's what will eventually happen to me."

"I don't care about catching the biggest fish or the most fish," he replied. "I just like to catch fish. And if I lose a couple hooks or have a tangled mess in my tackle box along the way, well, that's all part of the fishing experience. Look, if you go fishing with me this weekend, I think you'll understand. Do you want to come? Who knows? Maybe you'll get some more content for another book."

I almost said yes, but only because of his last statement. It was true that I wanted to start writing a second book. But I knew that writing a book was only ten percent of the work. To truly be successful as an author, you have to market the book. So I declined his invitation, and went back to my study to plan my book tour and how I was going to give a TED talk about fishing.

If you are reading this book and want to become a famous fisherman like me, let me close out with a bit of advice. I encourage you to follow my example in becoming a famous fisherman. You must follow many of the same steps I did, one of which includes buying and reading books about fishing. Like this one. This book is a step in the right direction, and I hope that when my next book comes out, you will buy and read it as well.

Until then, remember that fishing is not about how many fish you catch, or even if you catch any fish at all. Being a fisherman is about learning how to fish. And as long as you are learning how to fish, you're headed in the right direction, even if you never catch any fish. So keep your hook in the water ... and out of your skin. (To be safe, all you really need to do is put a hook in a little cup of water.)

DISCUSSION QUESTIONS

Thank you for reading this satirical book on evangelism. I hope you enjoyed yourself, laughed a bit, and learned something along the way! As you read, you might have recognized some of the silly evangelistic situations from your own life or the life of others.

You might also be wondering how I came up with some of these ideas, and how many of them actually happened to me. (The answer is … more than you might imagine … though not the situation with the hooker.)

If you want some inside information on each chapter, join my online discipleship group and take the course titled "Adventures in Fishing for Men." Each lesson contains an audio recording of the chapter, a PDF download of the chapter, and a video of myself and my wife discussing the chapter and providing some suggestions on how to become a true "fisher of men." Go to RedeemingGod.com/join/ to sign up today. I look forward to seeing you there!

In the meantime, this study guide contains some suggested topics and questions you can use in a small group setting to discuss the content of each chapter and learn from the mistakes that many Christians make when trying to evangelize others. Many of the questions are only rhetorical, inviting you to think about the message of the chapter and how you might have misunderstood the goals of evangelism.

1. THE KEY TO FISHING

In the story, what do you think the fishing gear represents? The boat? The magazines? Which of these things were necessary to actually start fishing? Why do you think the man purchased them? What sort of parallels do you see in modern church and evangelistic practices?

Why is there sometimes a connection in Christianity between evangelism and spending large amounts of money? Where did this connection come from? How and why is it encouraged?

When it comes to the money spent on "evangelism," might there be a better way of spending this money that might actually help love and serve those in your community? What are some of these ways?

The lesson and video for this chapter are found at:
https://redeeminggod.com/courses/fishing-for-
men/lessons/chapter-01/

2. MY FIRST DAY ON THE WATER

Many Christians talk about being "present" or "incarna-
tional" in their community so they can develop friendships with the people who live there. Do you think that
having a church building helps or hinders this community "presence"?

In this story, the man feels like he needs to "speak the
truth" to his neighbor about his wife. Have you ever
encountered a situation where some Christians said
something mean about you or someone else, but justi-
fied their words because they were just "speaking the
truth"? Why do you think we Christians feel we have
the right to speak the "truth" to people, even when it
hurts?

While we should always seek to "speak the truth in love"
(Eph 4:15), if you had to choose just one or the other,
which do you think is more helpful to others? Speaking
the truth in an unloving way or showing love in a way
that hides or masks the truth?

When hard and difficult truths need to be said, what is the best context for saying them? Read Proverbs 27:6 for some direction.

The lesson and video for this chapter are found at: https://redeeminggod.com/courses/fishing-for-men/lessons/chapter-02/

3. STOCKING UP ON FISH

Why do you think so many churches spend so much time and money getting non-believers into their church building? Is the church building and church service a safe and natural environment in which to build friendships with others? Why or why not?

Rather than try to build friendships with people during a few scripted and scheduled hours on Sunday morning in a church building, what are some ways and locations that might be more natural and effective for building true friendships with others?

Do you think that quoting Bible verses at people is a good way to reveal God's love and truth to them, especially if the other person is not a Christian and doesn't recognize the authority of Scripture? What might be a better way?

Have you ever been on the receiving end of a "Bible Verse Barrage" where someone quotes Bible verses at you in an attempt to correct your beliefs or behaviors? Relate this story to others and how it made you feel.

What are some of the possible reasons that Christians quote Bible verses at others? Is it because they don't know what else to say? Are they trying to "win" the conversation by quoting the ultimate authority, God? Are they trying to show how smart they are?

Why do you think that Christians who quote Bible verses at others most often choose Bible verses which portray God as a vengeful, judging, condemning, and angry God? Is there a connection between how they view God, the Bible verses they choose to quote, and the way they treat other people?

People who quote Bible verses at others often respond negatively with bullying-tactics or name-calling when others do not respond positively to the Bible quotations. Why do you think this occurs?

Why do some Christians feel that justice is accomplished by getting others fired from their job? Is this really a good way of spreading the gospel of love and grace? Why or why not?

The lesson and video for this chapter are found at: https://redeeminggod.com/courses/fishing-for-men/lessons/chapter-03/

4.   FISHING SCIENCE

Why do you think some Christians are happy to consign others to everlasting torment in hell? Do you think that this attitude is a proper reflection of the heart of God, or does it say something instead about the heart of humanity?

In the story, the man misunderstands something he read in one of his magazines about fish hiding behind rocks and trees. Do Christians ever misunderstand something they read about in one of their books ... or in the Bible itself? Do you think that any modern Christian theology or church practices ever developed from these misunderstandings? If so, what?

Do Christians ever suffer from selective hearing when it comes to science and history, accepting only what confirms and supports our presuppositions, rather than allowing the sciences to challenge and change our views? How does the man in the story do this, and what are some parallels in modern church culture?

Which is worse … bad words or bad behavior? Why do you think some Christians are so offended by bad words even though they engage in some of the worst possible behaviors?

After the man in the story tears up his neighbor's lawn, he apologizes. But is it a real apology? Why or why not? What does a real apology consist of? Do you think that Christians need to apologize to the world for anything? If so, what, and how can we best apologize to them?

The lesson and video for this chapter are found at: https://redeeminggod.com/courses/fishing-for-men/lessons/chapter-04/

5. HOW TO ATTRACT FISH

Many Christians fail to see their own faults, while often pointing out the faults in others. And often, when Christians find themselves in conflict with others, they fail to see how they contributed to that conflict. What are some ways we can start to have our eyes opened to our own faults and how we cause conflict with other people?

Have you ever seen a website which contains pictures of silly church signs? (If you want to see some, just do a Google search.) Have you ever known anyone who started attending a church because of their sign? More often than not, people just roll their eyes at these signs. So why do we still try to use church signs as an evangelistic tactic?

Church signs are not the only marketing tactic churches use when trying to invite others to their services. There are mass mailings, radio ads, TV commercials, and all sorts of other gimmicky ways churches try to get more people in the pews. Why do we engage in these practices, when they tend to do more harm than good to our message and mission? Might there be some more friendly and personable ways to let people know who we are and what we stand for?

Churches spend lots of time and money on advertising and marketing in an attempt to get people to visit and attend their Sunday service. What do you think might happen if this same time and money were used instead to help the community in tangible ways? Would this be more or less effective?

The lesson and video for this chapter are found at:
https://redeeminggod.com/courses/fishing-for-
men/lessons/chapter-05/

6. THE FISHIN' MISSION

It is not uncommon to hear about seminars or conferences that promise to teach Christians about the values
and goals of the unchurched as a way of attracting them
to church. But have you ever heard of a seminar or
training for learning about the values and goals of people who might be your friends? Of course not. If you
have to study and analyze the sorts of people who might
be your friends, then whomever you find through this
process will not be your friend. The analysis ruins the
friendship. So why do we approach evangelism this way
in the church?

The same goes for door-to-door evangelism and wind-
shield flyers. Nobody ever developed a relationship with
such tactics, so why does the church try to use these in
some of our forms of evangelism?

When God calls us to go somewhere with Him, why do
we often spend more time telling others about what we

are going to do, and asking for them to pray for us, than actually *doing* what God called us to do?

When God calls us to serve Him in some way, why do we often think that God must also be calling others to do the same thing, and that it is our job to ask them to join us? Could it be that God has called them to do something else, and if they join us, then they will be failing to do what God has called them to do? Is it possible that we try to recruit help because it gains attention for us from others while also keeping us from actually obeying God?

The lesson and video for this chapter are found at: https://redeeminggod.com/courses/fishing-for-men/lessons/chapter-06/

7. MY TRIP TO THE RIVER

In this chapter, the man knew nothing about the fishermen floating down the river, but he still condemned them for being false fishermen, when in reality, they were the only ones actually fishing. Have ever seen something like this happen in Christian circles?

A favorite Christian pastime is judging, condemning, and criticizing others who do not dress like them, look like them, or act like them. Why do you think this is? Do you think this behavior is more or less common within Christian circles? Why do you think this is?

Why do many Christians seem to think that "book knowledge" gained at Seminary and Bible College is better than practical knowledge gained through life and real-world experiences?

The lesson and video for this chapter are found at: https://redeeminggod.com/courses/fishing-for-men/lessons/chapter-07/

8. HOOKED ON FISHING

This chapter introduces the idea that the man's neighbor seems to know something about fishing. But the man is too suspicious and proud to consider suggestions or accept advice. As a result, he gets hurt in the process of practicing his casting technique. Why do you think that so many Christians are hesitant to accept the advice or suggestions of other, more experienced people when these other people are non-Christians?

When the man gets a hook stuck in his ear, he blames his neighbor, even after the neighbor had warned him against using the hook. Why are some Christians so quick to blame others when things go wrong in the world or in their life, especially when we ignored the experienced advice of other people?

The lesson and video for this chapter are found at: https://redeeminggod.com/courses/fishing-for-men/lessons/chapter-08/

9. AN EXPENSIVE LESSON IN HOOKING

Many Christians are completely ignorant of the world they want to reach. As a result, they often engage in offensive practices and behavior that does more damage than good to the cause of Christ. How can Christians learn more about this world and the people in it that we want to reach without engaging in the sinful practices? (And no, the answer is *not* to read books about the world or attend more seminars.)

The Gospels record that Jesus hung out with sinners, tax collectors, and prostitutes. They further record Jesus' opinion that these "sinners" were closer to the kingdom of God than were religious people. What do you think He meant? Several years back, I wrote an article on this topic: https://redeeminggod.com/jesus-the-friend-of-sinners/ Read and discuss.

The lesson and video for this chapter are found at: https://redeeminggod.com/courses/fishing-for-men/lessons/chapter-09/

10. LETTING OTHERS KNOW YOU FISH

Christianity is full of "professionals" who teach others to do what they themselves have not done and cannot do. But which would you rather learn from: Someone who has studied all the books and knows all the latest theories and approaches to what they teach, or someone who actually *does* what they teach? Why?

Why do you think there is such a large market for Christian t-shirts, bumper stickers, and jewelry? Which is a better evangelistic strategy: letting people know we are Christians by what we wear, or letting people know we are Christians by our love?

I once read that the average church conversion rate was less than 1% per year. In other words, for every 100 people in the church, less than one person became a new Christian each year. Yet the church rarely changes its strategy or approach to sharing the gospel with the world, but only doubles down on the failed approaches of the past. Why do you think the church continues to pour more money and effort into these failed approaches? What is the alternative?

The lesson and video for this chapter are found at: https://redeeminggod.com/courses/fishing-for-men/lessons/chapter-10/

11. FISHING RITES

Many Christians do not know or understand where many of our Christian rites (such as baptism and communion) come from, or why we do them the way we do. The same thing is true of most church traditions. But they keep doing them anyway. Why do you think this happens and what can we do about it? (My 5-book "Close Your Church for Good" book series seeks to address many of these traditions and propose alternative practices.)

In this chapter, what Christian ritual does net washing represent, and what are the parallels between net washing and this Christian ritual? What about eating fish crackers and drinking fish water?

Have you noticed how the man in the story takes figurative and symbolic ideas (such as the idea that he should eat, drink, and breathe fishing) and attempts to interpret and apply them literally? Can you think of any practices within Christianity that does the same thing?

Do the traditions and actions we do as "devoted Christians" really make us better Christians? Do these traditions help us live and love like Jesus in this world? Why or why not? Are there things we could be doing instead that would better reflect Jesus to this world?

The lesson and video for this chapter are found at: https://redeeminggod.com/courses/fishing-for-men/lessons/chapter-11/

12. MEETING FISH NEEDS

There is a popular movement in Christianity about need-oriented evangelism. It considers the needs and goals of unchurched people, and then seeks to build the ministries and meetings of the church around those needs. Many churches have grown quite large as a result of this approach. But can you think of any drawbacks with this approach to ministry?

When we approach other people in need-oriented fashion, we are trying to get them to join us in what we are doing. Do you think that ministry might work better if we joined them in what they were doing? Why or why not?

If we really want to learn about the goals, desires, needs, and problems of the unchurched, is there a better way of learning about this than performing surveys and reading studies? What are some of these ways?

Some Christians take great pride in being "strange" for Jesus. There is even a name for it: It's called being a "Jesus Freak." Such people are proud of acting different, talking different, dressing different, and behaving different than everyone else, and often, they are quite judgmental and rude toward everyone else. But historical reports of the early Christians say that you could not tell a Christian apart from anyone else on the street through their clothing, habits, or speech. The only thing that separated early Christians from everyone else was their love. How can Christians start living this same way today?

The lesson and video for this chapter are found at: https://redeeminggod.com/courses/fishing-for-men/lessons/chapter-12/

13. THE FISHING CHANNEL

This chapter clearly has TBN (Trinity Broadcasting Network) in view. This Christian television channel would be pure comedy if it weren't so sad. Why do you think this channel exists, what do you think it accomplishes for the gospel (good or bad), and why do you think some Christians spend so much time (and money) watching it?

Read the chapter again, and consider the various types of lies and deceptions that are taught by the teachers on TBN to the viewing audience.

What is the attraction to giving money to pastors or teachers so that *they* can perform the ministry for us? Is there a different way this money could be used in our own local communities?

The lesson and video for this chapter are found at: https://redeeminggod.com/courses/fishing-for-men/lessons/chapter-13/

14. ATTENDING THE FISHING CLUB

Did you know that "church" is not something you can attend? When we understand what the church actually *is,* it is impossible to "go to church." Since the church is the family of God, you can no more "attend a church" then you can "attend a family." So why is there so much emphasis in Christianity today on attending church?

When Christians meet each other for the first time, one of the first questions we ask is, "So where do you attend church?" Why is this?

If a person stops "attending church," why do we feel like they have "fallen away" from the faith, or abandoned Jesus?

Think about the amount of time you spend each week at church or planning and preparing for church-related activities. Also include things like Bible studies and prayer groups. Do such things really "serve God"? What other ways could you use this same amount of time to better serve God and others in this world?

The lesson and video for this chapter are found at: https://redeeminggod.com/courses/fishing-for-men/lessons/chapter-14/

15. LEARNING THE LINGO

Notice how now that the man is living in his garage and is not able to watch his favorite shows on television, he decides that watching television is a waste of time, and nobody else should watch it either. Have you ever encountered Christians who make rules for everybody else based on what they themselves cannot do? If so, what happened?

What is the fascination in some Christian circles with using big words and fancy terminology? Do such terms really help us understand or live the gospel? Do these words better help us connect with or love non-Christians? Do they aid us in understanding the pain, sorrow, and frustrations that real people feel in the real world?

Have you ever heard of the "Christian Bubble"? What does this term mean to you, how can it be recognized, and what sort of steps can be taken to make sure that we are not living in it?

When was the last time you shopped in a Christian bookstore? Was the description in this chapter fairly true to what you found in that store? Specifically, how much of the Christian bookstore was devoted to books, and how much was devoted to knick-knacks? Do you know why Christian bookstores devote so much space to items other than books? What does this tell you about the state of modern Christianity?

The lesson and video for this chapter are found at: https://redeeminggod.com/courses/fishing-for-men/lessons/chapter-15/

16. THE FISHING TRAINING CONFERENCE

Have you ever attended an Evangelism Training Conference? Most Christians have. Were you better at evangelism after the conference than before? Most Christians are not. Do you remember much of what you learned at this conference? Probably not. So why do we have these conferences? What is their actual purpose?

Now think of a time when you actually served a needy person, or loved someone in your neighborhood in a tangible way. Was this a positive experience? How did you feel afterwards? Did it encourage you to love and serve others more? Have you been loving and serving others more since this experience?

Why does it often seem that many of the books, trainings, and activities we offer Christians to help them evangelize and serve the world only gets in the way of people actually serving the world? And since such activities are so ineffective at what they claim to accomplish, why do Christians keep doing them?

Do you recognize any of the seminar trainings that the man attends as being related to actual evangelism trainings that are available in the Christian marketplace today? If so, which ones?

The lesson and video for this chapter are found at: https://redeeminggod.com/courses/fishing-for-men/lessons/chapter-16/

17. THE FISHING PRAYER

Some Christians believe that prayer consists of reciting the Lord's Prayer once or twice a day. Do you think this is why Jesus gave us this prayer? If not, what was the purpose of the Lord's Prayer, and how are we to pray instead?

Have you ever encountered Christians who use prayer as a weapon? They might be offering "prayer requests" when they are actually gossiping. Or they promise to pray for someone's problems instead of actually doing something about those problems. Or they use prayer as a way of publicly correcting or shaming someone. Or as a way to seem pious and holy in the eyes of other people (cf. Matt 6:5-8). What are your thoughts and experiences will all these sorts of prayers?

Jesus was the most effective "evangelist" the world has ever seen, and He spent lots of time in prayer. What is the connection between prayer and evangelism?

The lesson and video for this chapter are found at: https://redeeminggod.com/courses/fishing-for-men/lessons/chapter-17/

18. STRATEGIC HELP IN TRAINING PEOPLE TO LOVE ANGLING NOW

Does your church have a Mission Statement? A Purpose Statement? A set of core values? A Doctrinal Statement? A Membership Code of Conduct Statement? A 5-year and 10-year plan? A constitution? If you answered "Yes" to any of these, do you know what the statement says?

Were you part of the committee that came up with one of these statements? How much time and energy was spent on drafting and approving them? Do you think this was a good use of time and energy? What effects (positive and negative) do these statements have on the ability of the people in the church to love and serve others?

Since all these plans and statements accomplish so little in the actual goal and mission of the church, why do some churches spend so much time and energy crafting and talking about them?

The lesson and video for this chapter are found at: https://redeeminggod.com/courses/fishing-for-men/lessons/chapter-18/

19. FISHING IN AFRICA

Which person do you think would make a better missionary to Africa? Here are the choices: An English-speaking American with a Master's degree who needs to raise a hundred thousand dollars per year to support his western lifestyle in a poor African country and also return home on a regular basis for medical needs and fundraising efforts, *or* a native-born African with little education who understand the culture and the people of Africa and who is willing to live among the people to whom he ministers and can be fully supported for a few thousand dollars per year.

Why do we spend hundreds of thousands of dollars to train and send a missionary to a foreign country when we have trouble spending much smaller amounts of money to love and serve people in our home towns?

If someone has a poor track record of ministering to people in their own community, would this be a good person to support for ministry overseas? Why or why not?

Why do many western missionaries think that churches and Christians in third-word countries need to follow and adopt the same practices and traditions that are mostly ineffective in our own culture? Do poor communities in Africa or Asia really need expensive buildings and baptismals, along with professionally-trained clergy to lead the services? Why or why not?

The lesson and video for this chapter are found at: https://redeeminggod.com/courses/fishing-for-men/lessons/chapter-19/

20. WORLD FISHING TRAINING CENTER

Why do you think that Christians put missionaries up on a pedestal?

Why does the church spend billions of dollars to teach people the Bible for "ministry," while failing to teach these newly-minted Bible experts how to love people like Jesus? Is there something lacking in our Christian education system, or is it a problem with higher education itself?

Have you ever known a Bible scholar or professional theologian who could interact well and easily connect with non-Christians? If so, who was it? If not, why do you think this is?

What is this chapter teaching about the story of the Widow's Mite in Luke 21:1-4? After reading this chapter, read that story again from Luke, and see if you read it with new eyes. The following article might also help: https://redeeminggod.com/devouring-widows-houses/

The lesson and video for this chapter are found at: https://redeeminggod.com/courses/fishing-for-men/lessons/chapter-20/

21. THE FISHING COVENANT

When some Christians fail to live as other Christians think they should, the temptation is to think that those Christians who "failed" weren't actually Christians in the first place. But do you think there might be a different explanation? If so, what is it?

What was Jesus most known for? Was it His doctrinal precision and insistence on proper behavior? Or was it His love and acceptance of all people? What did Jesus say about how others will know we are His disciples (John 13:35)?

Many Christians try to keep themselves from being "polluted by the world." As a result, they limit any real contact with non-Christians to a bare minimum. What does this form of living do to our ability to build friendships with others? Is it possible that this way of segregating ourselves from others is actually itself a sign of being polluted by a shattered and splintered world? Why or why not?

The lesson and video for this chapter are found at: https://redeeminggod.com/courses/fishing-for-men/lessons/chapter-21/

22. JOE THE FISHERMAN

The actions we are most critical of in others are often the things that we ourselves our guilty of committing. What do you often judge and condemn in other people? Are you guilty of something similar? Don't answer too quickly!

Why is full-time professional ministry so damaging to friendships and marriages? If you know a pastor's family that appears happy, you probably don't know them as well as you think. Those who claim to teach others to love often have trouble loving those in their own home. What does this say about the state of the church today?

Many Christians don't even know the names of their neighbors. If evangelism involves building friendships, then learning a person's name is the first step in evangelism. How can we try to reach the world with the gospel when we cannot even learn the names of our neighbors?

The lesson and video for this chapter are found at: https://redeeminggod.com/courses/fishing-for-men/lessons/chapter-22/

23. THE FISHING CHARADE

In this chapter, the man accuses Joe and his friends of being fake fisherman, just putting on a fishing charade to ruin him and his reputation. But who is really putting on the charade? Does it ever seem to you that most of what goes on in a church is a charade? If so, then who are the true followers of Jesus?

As you think through the Gospel accounts, who did Jesus praise as being closest to the kingdom of heaven, and therefore, most representative of His values, goals, and vision for this world? Where are such people today? If you want to love and serve others as Jesus wants for people in His kingdom, how can you go about starting to hang out with them where they're at?

Some people are afraid to interact with "sinners" in the world. But when we truly understand Jesus and the good news He brought, we have nothing to fear from them. What should we fear instead? What causes the man in the story to be blinded to the truth that is all around him? Is this similar to what caused the blindness of the religious rulers in the days of Jesus? If you think you might be blind in similar ways, how can you start learning to see again?

The lesson and video for this chapter are found at: https://redeeminggod.com/courses/fishing-for-men/lessons/chapter-23/

24. BECOMING A PUBLISHED FISHERMAN

Why do we determine the worth or value of a pastor by the books and articles the pastor writes, the conferences and seminars the pastor teaches, or the size of the church the pastor leads? What are some more Christlike standards that could be used to determine the quality of spiritual leadership a pastor provides?

In the beginning of the book, the man wanted to become a great fisherman, and the evidence of this would be if he caught fish. But now, at the end of the book, he considers himself a great fisherman because he wrote a book about fishing and people read it. But he still hasn't caught any fish. Can you think of ways that Christians "move the goal posts" in similar ways to make themselves look successful, when in fact, they are dismal failures as far as the gospel is concerned?

Does it ever seem that Christianity is mostly about a never-ending cycle of learning? Or that the main truth you learn is how much more you need to learn? Let me tell you a secret: You know more than enough. Truly. So just get out there and start loving people. Truly loving them, with no strings attached, and no hidden agendas. Then you will become like Jesus and will truly be living the gospel in this wonderful world.

The lesson and video for this chapter are found at: https://redeeminggod.com/courses/fishing-for-men/lessons/chapter-24/

FIRECRACKER FISH

This recipe was learned from "Shorty" after my wife and I went lake trout charter fishing on Flathead Lake in Bigfork, Montana. If you ever visit Flathead Lake, watch out for the Flathead Lake Monster!

Ingredients:
- 2 Large Lake Trout Fillets
- 1 Tbsp White Wine

Mix all the following together in a bowl:
- 2 Tbsp Olive Oil
- 1 Tbsp Lemon Juice
- 16 Black Olives, Sliced
- 6 Green Olives, Sliced
- ½ Cup Chopped Cilantro
- ¼ Cup Sundried Tomatoes
- ⅓ Cup Salted Peanuts

Instructions:

Line a pan with foil and add mixture of ingredients to the pan. Put fish on top of mixture, and then drizzle the white wine onto the fish. Bake at 350° for 20-30 minutes, and then transfer to the top rack and broil for 5-10 minutes. When you serve, put the fish on the plate first, and then the mixture on top of the fish.

ABOUT JEREMY MYERS

Jeremy Myers is an author, blogger, podcaster, and Bible teacher who lives in Oregon with his wife and three daughters. He primarily writes at RedeemingGod.com, where he seeks to help liberate people from the shackles of religion. He also hosts an online discipleship group where hundreds of like-minded people discuss life and theology and encourage each other to follow Jesus into the world.

If you appreciated the content of this book, would you consider recommending it to your friends and leaving a review on Amazon? Thanks!

JOIN JEREMY MYERS AND LEARN MORE

Take Bible and theology courses by joining Jeremy at
RedeemingGod.com/join/
Receive updates about free books, discounted books, and new books by joining Jeremy at
RedeemingGod.com/read-books/

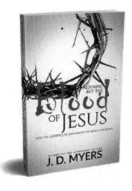

NOTHING BUT THE BLOOD OF JESUS: HOW THE SACRIFICE OF JESUS SAVES THE WORLD FROM SIN

Do you have difficulties reconciling God's behavior in the Old Testament with that of Jesus in the New?

Do you find yourself trying to rationalize God's violent demeanor in the Bible to unbelievers or even to yourself?

Does it seem disconcerting that God tells us not to kill others but He then takes part in some of the bloodiest wars and vindictive genocides in history?

The answer to all such questions is found in Jesus on the cross. By focusing your eyes on Jesus Christ and Him crucified, you come to understand that God was never angry at human sinners, and that no blood sacrifice was ever needed to purchase God's love, forgiveness, grace, and mercy.

In *Nothing but the Blood of Jesus*, J. D. Myers shows how the death of Jesus on the cross reveals the truth about the five concepts of sin, law, sacrifice, scapegoating, and bloodshed. After carefully defining each, this book shows how these definitions provide clarity on numerous biblical texts.

REVIEWS FROM AMAZON

> Building on his previous book, 'The Atonement of God', the work of René Girard and a solid grounding in the Scriptures, Jeremy Myers shares fresh and challenging insights with us about sin, law, sacrifice, scapegoating and blood. This book reveals to us how truly precious the blood of Jesus is and the way of escaping the cycle of blame, rivalry, scapegoating, sacrifice and violence that has plagued humanity since the time of Cain and Abel. 'Nothing but the Blood of Jesus' is an important and timely literary contribution to a world desperately in need of the non-violent message of Jesus.–Wesley Rostoll

> My heart was so filled with joy while reading this book. Jeremy you've reminded me once more that as you walk with Jesus and spend time in His presence, He talks to you and reveals Himself through the Scriptures. –Amazon Reader

Purchase the eBook for $5.99
Purchase the Paperback for $14.99

THE ATONEMENT OF GOD: BUILDING YOUR THEOLOGY ON A CRUCIVISION OF GOD

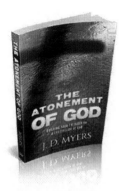

After reading this book, you will never read the Bible the same way again.

By reading this book, you will learn to see God in a whole new light. You will also learn to see yourself in a whole new light, and learn to live life in a whole new way.

The book begins with a short explanation of the various views of the atonement, including an explanation and defense of the "Non-Violent View" of the atonement. This view argues that God did not need or demand the death of Jesus in order to forgive sins. In fact, God has never been angry with us at all, but has always loved and always forgiven.

Following this explanation of the atonement, J. D. Myers takes you on a journey through 10 areas of theology which are radically changed and transformed by the Non-Violent view of the atonement. Read this book, and let your life and theology look more and more like Jesus Christ!

Outstanding book! Thank you for helping me understand "Crucivision" and the "Non-Violent Atonement." Together, they help it all make sense and fit so well into my personal thinking about God. I am encouraged to be truly free to love and forgive, because God has always loved and forgiven without condition, because Christ exemplified this grace on the Cross, and because the Holy Spirit is in the midst of all life, continuing to show the way through people like you. –Samuel R. Mayer

This book gives another view of the doctrines we have been taught all of our lives. And this actually makes more sense than what we have heard. I myself have had some of these thoughts but couldn't quite make the sense of it all by myself. J.D. Myers helped me answer some questions and settle some confusion for my doctrinal views. This is truly a refreshing read. Jesus really is the demonstration of who God is and God is much easier to understand than being so mean and vindictive in the Old Testament. The tension between the wrath of God and His justice and the love of God are eased when reading this understanding of the atonement. Read with an open mind and enjoy! –Clare N. Bez

Purchase the eBook for $4.99
Purchase the Paperback for $11.99

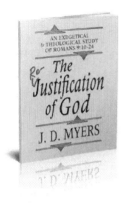

THE RE-JUSTIFICATION OF GOD: A STUDY OF ROMANS 9:10-24

Romans 9 has been a theological battleground for centuries. Scholars from all perspectives have debated whether Paul is teaching corporate or individual election, whether or not God truly hates Esau, and how to understand the hardening of Pharaoh's heart. Both sides have accused the other of misrepresenting God.

In this book, J. D. Myers presents a mediating position. Gleaning from both Calvinistic and Arminian insights into Romans 9, J. D. Myers presents a beautiful portrait of God as described by the pen of the Apostle Paul.

Here is a way to read Romans 9 which allows God to remain sovereign and free, but also allows our theology to avoid the deterministic tendencies which have entrapped certain systems of the past.

Read this book and—maybe for the first time—learn to see God the way Paul saw Him.

Fantastic read! Jeremy Myers has a gift for seeing things from outside of the box and making it easy to understand for the rest of us. The Re-Justification of God provides a fresh and insightful look into Romans 9:10-24 by interpreting it within the context of chapters 9-11 and then fitting it into the framework of Paul's entire epistle as well. Jeremy manages to provide a solid theological exegesis on a widely misunderstood portion of scripture without it sounding to academic. Most importantly, it provides us with a better view and understanding of who God is. If I had a list of ten books that I thought every Christian should read, this one would be on the list. –Wesley Rostoll

I loved this book! It made me cry and fall in love with God all over again. Romans is one of my favorite books, but now my eyes have been opened to what Paul was really saying. I knew in my heart that God was the good guy, but J. D. Myers provided the analysis to prove the text. ... I can with great confidence read the difficult chapters of Romans, and my furrowed brow is eased. Thank you, J. D. Myers. I love God, even more and am so grateful that his is so longsuffering in his perfect love! Well done. –Treinhart

Purchase the eBook for $2.99
Purchase the Paperback for $9.99

WHAT IS PRAYER? HOW TO PRAY TO GOD THE WAY YOU TALK TO A FRIEND

Stop worrying about how to pray, and just start praying! This book reveals the simple truth that you already know how to pray.

Once you know how to pray as discussed in this book, you will also discover that you already know what to pray for and how to see more answers to your prayers.

Read this book and find the freedom and power in your prayer life you have always longed for.

This book is Volume #1 in the Christian Questions Book Series by J. D. Myers, in which everyday questions from Christians are given down-to-earth answers from author and Bible teacher, Jeremy Myers.

REVIEWS FROM AMAZON

Jeremy's first chapter on "How To Talk To God" is so freeing. Talking to best friends is easy for most. Jeremy encourages us to not complicate matters and simply talk to God like you would a good friend who cares about you. The second chapter has some great illustrations and follows up from the first chapter – prayer is just having a conversation than having to worry about a script or what to say. –Mike Edwards, writing at "What God May Really be Like"

I love this book! J.D. Myers has done such a great job of putting into clear words all the things about prayer that have been developing in my thoughts for years. If you wonder what praying means, if you wonder what praying should be like, or even if you wonder why on earth people should even pray, read this. This is, so far, my favorite Jeremy Myers book. Not too deep, not too theological, not even too serious—though the subject matter is serious and is dealt with seriously. The tone of the writing is perfect, Excellent book. –B Shuford

Jeremy Myers beautifully unpacks what prayer is and how to pray naturally to God in this new book. As usual it is well written and easy to read and comprehend. I found it to clarify and expand my understanding of prayer and how to pray. Thanks Jeremy Myers for another exceptional book! I highly recommend this book to help anyone wanting to learn how to comfortably pray and actually enjoy prayer time. –Jim Maus

Purchase the eBook for $3.99
Purchase the Paperback for $9.99

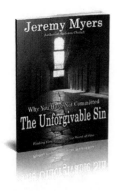

WHY YOU HAVE NOT COMMITTED THE UNFORGIVABLE SIN: FINDING FORGIVENESS FOR THE WORST OF SINS

Are you afraid that you have committed the unforgivable sin?

In this book, you will learn what this sin is and why you have not committed it. After surveying the various views about blasphemy against the Holy Spirit and examining Matthew 12:31-32, you will learn what the sin is and how it is committed.

As a result of reading this book, you will gain freedom from the fear of committing the worst of all sins, and learn how much God loves you!

REVIEWS FROM AMAZON

This book addressed things I have struggled and felt pandered to for years, and helped to bring wholeness to my heart again. –Natalie Fleming

A great read, on a controversial subject; biblical, historical and contextually treated to give the greatest understanding. May be the best on this subject (and there is very few) ever written. – Tony Vance

You must read this book. Forgiveness is necessary to see your blessings. So if you purchase this book, [you will have] no regrets. –Virtuous Woman

Jeremy Myers covers this most difficult topic thoroughly and with great compassion. –J. Holland

Wonderful explication of the unpardonable sin. God loves you more than you know. May Jesus Christ be with you always. –Robert M Sawin III

Excellent book! Highly recommend for anyone who has anxiety and fear about having committed the unforgivable sin. –William Tom

As someone who is constantly worried that they have disappointed or offended God, this book was, quite literally, a "Godsend." I thought I had committed this sin as I swore against the Holy Spirit in my mind. It only started after reading the verse about it in the Bible. The swear words against Him came into my mind over and over and I couldn't seem to stop no matter how much I prayed. I was convinced I was going to hell and cried constantly. I was extremely worried and depressed. This book has allowed me to breathe again, to have hope again. Thank you, Jeremy. I will read and re-read. I believe this book was definitely God inspired. I only wish I had found it sooner. –Sue

Purchase the eBook for $5.99
Purchase the Paperback for $8.99

SKELETON CHURCH: A BARE-BONES DEFINITION OF CHURCH (PREFACE TO THE CLOSE YOUR CHURCH FOR GOOD BOOK SERIES)

The church has a skeleton which is identical in all types of churches. Unity and peace can develop in Christianity if we recognize this skeleton as the simple, bare-bones definition of church. But when we focus on the outer trappings—the skin, hair, and eye color, the clothes, the muscle tone, and other outward appearances—division and strife form within the church.

Let us return to the skeleton church and grow in unity once again.

REVIEWS FROM AMAZON

I worried about buying another book that aimed at reducing things to a simple minimum, but the associations of the author along with the price gave me reason to hope and means to see. I really liked this book. First, because it wasn't identical to what other simple church people are saying. He adds unique elements that are worth reading. Second, the size is small enough to read, think, and pray about without getting lost. –Abel Barba

In *Skeleton Church*, Jeremy Myers makes us rethink church. For Myers, the church isn't a style of worship, a row of pews, or even a building. Instead, the church is the people of God, which provides the basic skeletal structure of the church. The muscles, parts, and flesh of the church are how we carry Jesus' mission into our own neighborhoods in our own unique ways. This eBook will make you see the church differently. –Travis Mamone

This book gets back to the basics of the New Testament church—who we are as Christians and what our perspective should be in the world we live in today. Jeremy cuts away all the institutional layers of a church and gets to the heart of our purpose as Christians in the world we live in and how to affect the people around us with God heart and view in mind. Not a physical church in mind. It was a great book and I have read it twice now. – Vaughn Bender

The Skeleton Church ... Oh. My. Word. Why aren't more people reading this!? It was well-written, explained everything beautifully, and it was one of the best explanations of how God intended for church to be. Not to mention an easy read! The author took it all apart, the church, and showed us how it should be. He made it real. If you are searching to find something or someone to show you what God intended for the church, this is the book you need to read. –Ericka

Purchase the Paperback for $8.99
Purchase the eBook for $2.99

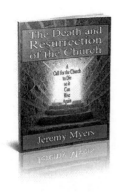

THE DEATH AND RESURRECTION OF THE CHURCH (VOLUME 1 IN THE CLOSE YOUR CHURCH FOR GOOD BOOK SERIES)

In a day when many are looking for ways to revitalize the church, Jeremy Myers argues that the church should die ... so that it can rise again.

This is not only because of the universal principle that death precedes resurrection, but also because the church has adopted certain Satanic values and goals and the only way to break free from our enslavement to these values is to die.

But death will not be the end of the church, just as death was not the end of Jesus. If the church follows Jesus into death, and even to the hellish places on earth, it is only then that the church will rise again to new life and vibrancy in the Kingdom of God.

REVIEWS FROM AMAZON

I have often thought on the church and how its acceptance of corporate methods and assimilation of cultural media mores taints its mission but Jeremy Myers eloquently captures in words the true crux of the matter—

that the church is not a social club for do-gooders but to disseminate the good news to all the nooks and crannies in the world and particularly and primarily those bastions in the reign of evil. That the "gates of Hell" Jesus pronounces indicate that the church is in an offensive, not defensive, posture as gates are defensive structures.

I must confess that in reading I was inclined to be in agreement as many of the same thinkers that Myers riffs upon have influenced me also—Walter Wink, Robert Farrar Capon, Greg Boyd, NT Wright, etc. So as I read, I frequently nodded my head in agreement. –GN Trifanaff

The book is well written, easy to understand, organized and consistent thoughts. It rightfully makes the reader at least think about things as … is "the way we have always done it" necessarily the Biblical or Christ-like way, or is it in fact very sinful?! I would recommend the book for pastors and church officers; those who have the most moving-and-shaking clout to implement changes, or keep things the same. –Joel M. Wilson

Absolutely phenomenal. Unless we let go of everything Adamic in our nature, we cannot embrace anything Christlike. For the church to die, we the individual temples must dig our graves. It is a must read for all who take issues about the body of Christ seriously. –Mordecai Petersburg

Purchase the eBook for $3.99
Purchase the Paperback for $8.99

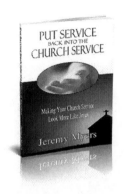

PUT SERVICE BACK INTO THE CHURCH SERVICE (VOLUME 2 IN THE CLOSE YOUR CHURCH FOR GOOD BOOK SERIES)

Churches around the world are trying to revitalize their church services. There is almost nothing they will not try. Some embark on multi-million dollar building campaigns while others sell their buildings to plant home churches. Some hire celebrity pastors to attract crowds of people, while others hire no clergy so that there can be open sharing in the service.

Yet despite everything churches have tried, few focus much time, money, or energy on the one thing that churches are supposed to be doing: loving and serving others like Jesus.

Put Service Back into the Church Service challenges readers to follow a few simple principles and put a few ideas into practice which will help churches of all types and sizes make serving others the primary emphasis of a church service.

Jeremy challenges church addicts, those addicted to an unending parade of church buildings, church services, Bible studies, church programs and more to follow Jesus into our communities, communities filled with lonely, hurting people and BE the church, loving the people in our world with the love of Jesus. Do we need another training program, another seminar, another church building, a remodeled church building, more staff, updated music, or does our world need us, the followers of Jesus, to BE the church in the world? The book is well-written, challenging and a book that really can make a difference not only in our churches, but also and especially in our neighborhoods and communities. –Charles Epworth

I just finished *Put Service Back Into Church Service* by Jeremy Myers, and as with his others books I have read on the church, it was very challenging. For those who love Jesus, but are questioning the function of the traditional brick and mortar church, and their role in it, this is a must read. It may be a bit unsettling to the reader who is still entrenched in traditional "church," but it will make you think, and possibly re-evaluate your role in the church. Get this book, and all others on the church by Jeremy. –Ward Kelly

Purchase the eBook for $3.99
Purchase the Paperback for $8.99

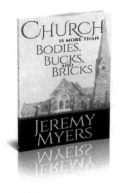

CHURCH IS MORE THAN BODIES, BUCKS, & BRICKS (VOLUME 3 IN THE CLOSE YOUR CHURCH FOR GOOD BOOK SERIES)

Many people define church as a place and time where people gather, a way for ministry money to be given and spent, and a building in which people regularly meet on Sunday mornings.

In this book, author and blogger Jeremy Myers shows that church is more than bodies, bucks, and bricks.

Church is the people of God who follow Jesus into the world, and we can be the church no matter how many people we are with, no matter the size of our church budget, and regardless of whether we have a church building or not.

By abandoning our emphasis on more people, bigger budgets, and newer buildings, we may actually liberate the church to better follow Jesus into the world.

REVIEWS FROM AMAZON

This book does more than just identify issues that have been bothering me about church as we know it, but it goes into history and explains how we got here. In this way it is similar to Viola's *Pagan Christianity*, but I found it a much more enjoyable read. Jeremy goes into more detail on the three issues he covers as well as giving a lot of practical advice on how to remedy these situations. – Portent

This book surprised me. I have never read anything from this author previously. The chapters on the evolution of the tithe were eye openers. This is something that has bothered me for years in the ministry. It may be truth that is too expensive to believe when it comes to feeding the monster. –Karl Ingersoll

Since I returned from Africa 20 years ago I have struggled with going to church back in the States. This book helped me not feel guilty and has helped me process this struggle. It is challenging and overflows with practical suggestions. He loves the church despite its imperfections and suggests ways to break the bondage we find ourselves in. –Truealian

Jeremy Meyers always writes a challenging book ... It seems the American church (as a whole) is very comfortable with the way things are ... The challenge is to get out of the brick and mortar buildings and stagnant programs and minister to the needy in person with funds in hand to meet their needs especially to the widows and orphans as we are directed in the scriptures. –GGTexas

Purchase the eBook for $3.99
Purchase the Paperback for $9.99

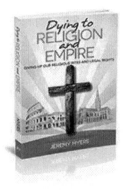

DYING TO RELIGION AND EMPIRE (VOLUME 4 IN THE CLOSE YOUR CHURCH FOR GOOD BOOK SERIES)

Could Christianity exist without religious rites or legal rights? In *Dying to Religion and Empire*, I not only answer this question with an emphatic "Yes!" but argue that if the church is going to thrive in the coming decades, we must give up our religious rites and legal rights.

Regarding religious rites, I call upon the church to abandon the quasi-magical traditions of water baptism and the Lord's Supper and transform or redeem these practices so that they reflect the symbolic meaning and intent which they had in New Testament times.

Furthermore, the church has become far too dependent upon certain legal rights for our continued existence. Ideas such as the right to life, liberty, and the pursuit of happiness are not conducive to living as the people of God who are called to follow Jesus into servanthood and death. Also, reliance upon the freedom of speech, the freedom of assembly, and other such freedoms as established by the Bill of Rights have made the church a servant of the state rather than a servant of God and the gospel. Such freedoms must be forsaken if we are going to live within the rule and reign of God on earth.

This book not only challenges religious and political liberals but conservatives as well. It is a call to leave behind the comfortable religion we know, and follow Jesus into the uncertain and wild ways of radical discipleship. To rise and live in the reality of God's Kingdom, we must first die to religion and empire.

REVIEWS FROM AMAZON

Jeremy is one of the freshest, freest authors out there— and you need to hear what he has to say. This book is startling and new in thought and conclusion. Are the "sacraments" inviolate? Why? Do you worship at a secular altar? Conservative? Liberal? Be prepared to open your eyes. Mr. Myers will not let you keep sleeping!

Jeremy Myers is one or the most thought provoking authors that I read, this book has really helped me to look outside the box and start thinking how can I make more sense of my relationship with Christ and how can I show others in a way that impacts them the way that Jesus' disciples impacted their world. Great book, great author. – Brett Hotchkiss

Purchase the eBook for $3.99
Purchase the Paperback for $9.99

CRUCIFORM PASTORAL LEADERSHIP (VOLUME 5 IN THE CLOSE YOUR CHURCH FOR GOOD BOOK SERIES)

This book is forthcoming in early 2017.

The final volume in the *Close Your Church for Good* book series look at issues related to pastoral leadership in the church. It discusses topics such as preaching and pastoral pay from the perspective of the cross.

The best way pastors can lead their church is by following Jesus to the cross!

This book will be published in 2018.

CHRISTMAS REDEMPTION: WHY CHRISTIANS SHOULD CELEBRATE A PAGAN HOLIDAY

Christmas Redemption looks at some of the symbolism and traditions of Christmas, including gifts, the Christmas tree, and even Santa Claus and shows how all of these can be celebrated and enjoyed by Christians as a true and accurate reflection of the gospel.

Though Christmas used to be a pagan holiday, it has been redeemed by Jesus.

If you have been told that Christmas is a pagan holiday and is based on the Roman festival of Saturnalia, or if you have been told that putting up a Christmas tree is idolatrous, or if you have been told that Santa Claus is Satanic and teaches children to be greedy, then you must read this book! In it, you will learn that all of these Christmas traditions have been redeemed by Jesus and are good and healthy ways of celebrating the truth of the gospel and the grace of Jesus Christ.

REVIEWS FROM AMAZON

Too many times we as Christians want to condemn nearly everything around us and in so doing become much like the Pharisees and religious leaders that Jesus encountered. I recommend this book to everyone who has concerns of how and why we celebrate Christmas. I recommend it to those who do not have any qualms in celebrating but may not know the history of Christmas. I recommend this book to everyone, no matter who or where you are, no matter your background or beliefs, no matter whether you are young or old. –David H.

Very informative book dealing with the roots of our modern Christmas traditions. The Biblical teaching on redemption is excellent! Highly recommended. –Tamara

This is a wonderful book full of hope and joy. The book explains where Christmas traditions originated and how they have been changed and been adapted over the years. The hope that the grace that is hidden in the celebrations will turn more hearts to the Lord's call is very evident. Jeremy Myers has given us a lovely gift this Christmas. His insights will lift our hearts and remain with us a long time. –Janet Cardoza

I love how the author uses multiple sources to back up his opinions. He doesn't just use bible verses, he goes back into the history of the topics (pagan rituals, Santa, etc.) as well. Great book! –Jenna G.

Purchase the eBook for $2.99

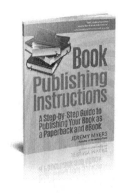

BOOK PUBLISHING INSTRUCTIONS: A STEP-BY-STEP GUIDE TO PUBLISHING YOUR BOOK AS A PAPERBACK AND EBOOK

The dirty little secret of the publishing industry is that authors don't really need publishing companies any longer. If you want to get published, you can!

This book gives you everything you need to take your unfinished manuscript and get it into print and into the hands of readers. It shows you how to format your manuscript for printing as a paperback and preparing the files for digital eReaders like the Kindle, iPad, and Nook.

This book provides tips and suggestions for editing and typesetting your book, inserting interior images, designing a book cover, and even marketing your book so that people will buy it and read it. Detailed descriptions of what to do are accompanied by screenshots for each step. Additional tools, tips, and websites are also provided which will help get your book published.

If you have a book idea, you need to read this book.

I self-published my first book with the "assistance" of a publishing company. In the end I was extremely unhappy for various reasons … Jeremy Myers' book … does not try to impress with all kinds of "learned quotations" but gets right to the thrust of things, plain and simple. For me this book will be a constant companion as I work on a considerable list of books on Christian doctrines. Whether you are a new aspiring author or one with a book or so behind you, save yourself much effort and frustration by investing in this book.
–Gerrie Malan

This book was incredibly helpful. I am in the process of writing my first book and the info in here has really helped me go into this process with a plan. I now realize how incredibly naive I was about what goes into publishing a book, yet instead of feeling overwhelmed, I now feel prepared for the task. Jeremy has laid out the steps to every aspect of publishing step by step as though they were recipes in a cook book. From writing with Styles and using the Style guide to incorporating images and page layouts, it is all there and will end up saving you hours of time in the editing phase. –W. Rostoll

Purchase the eBook for $9.99
Purchase the Paperback for $14.99

THE LIE – A SHORT STORY

When one billion people disappear from earth, what explanation does the president provide? Is he telling the truth, or exposing an age-old lie?

This fictional short story contains his televised speech.

Have you ever wondered what the antichrist will say when a billion people disappear from planet earth at the rapture? Here is a fictional account of what he might say.

Purchase the eBook for $0.99

JOIN JEREMY MYERS AND LEARN MORE

Take Bible and theology courses by joining Jeremy at
RedeemingGod.com/join/

Receive updates about free books, discounted books, and new books by joining Jeremy at
RedeemingGod.com/read-books/